Understanding Dyslexia

A Guide for Teachers and Parents

Denis Lawrence

 Open University Press

Open University Press
McGraw-Hill Education
McGraw-Hill House
Shoppenhangers Road
Maidenhead
Berkshire
England
SL6 2QL

Mixed Sources
Product group from well-managed
forests and other controlled sources
www.fsc.org Cert no. TT-COC-002769
© 1996 Forest Stewardship Council

email: enquiries@openup.co.uk
world wide web: www.openup.co.uk

and
Two Penn Plaza, New York, NY 10121-2289, USA

First published 2009

A catalogue record of this book is available from the British Library

ISBN10: 0 335 23594 8 (pb) 0 335 23595 6 (hb)
ISBN13: 978 0 335 23594 0 (pb) 978 0 335 23595 7 (hb)

Library of Congress Cataloging-in-Publication Data
CIP data has been applied for

Typeset by Aptara Inc., India
Printed in the UK by Bell and Bain Ltd, Glasgow

Fictitous names of companies, products, people, characters and/or data that
may be used herein (in case studies or in examples) are not intended to
represent any real individual, company, product or event.

Thinking Children was first published by the New Zealand Council for
Educational Research (NZCER Press) 1995.

The **McGraw·Hill** Companies

Acknowledgements

I became aware of the need for this book while assessing children with dyslexia and talking to their parents and to their teachers. It is to these adults and children that I wish to dedicate this book. It has been a privilege to meet them all and to share their fears and their hopes. There are too many of them to name them individually, but I would like to thank them all. Although parents and their children first stimulated me to write this book, it would not have been completed without the support of my wife, Anne. I must thank her wholeheartedly, not only for her sustained encouragement throughout the writing of the manuscript, but also for her help in its organization and editing. I thank her also for putting her computer skills at my disposal, without which the manuscript would still be unfinished. I am grateful also to my daughters, Diane and Helen, who provided me with useful information on the present state of dyslexia in schools. Finally, I owe a debt of gratitude to Fiona Richman, Commissioning Editor at the Open University Press, who had the foresight to see the need for this book.

Cover Photograph:

'Precious moments'

by

Dominic McKenna

Contents

List of tables

Introduction

Dyslexia has been a topic of debate for many decades and still continues to be a subject for discussion. During the early days of the debate many educationalists doubted the existence of dyslexia. At that time, there was more argument than research. Since those days research evidence has gradually accumulated to convince even the most hardened critic of the existence of dyslexia. There is little doubt that some children have difficulties with the learning of literacy skills, despite appropriate learning experiences. Also, there is some evidence to show that there are likely to be neurological and genetic bases for dyslexia, even if the precise roles played by genetics and neurology are not always clear.

Although most dyslexia appears to have a genetic base, in some cases environmental factors may be responsible. An extreme example of this would be where an accident has caused a brain injury and language facility is lost. In those instances, the difficulty would be referred to as secondary dyslexia, or acquired dyslexia.

Despite agreement on the existence of dyslexia and its likely origins, several questions remain unanswered. Foremost among these questions is, how should we define dyslexia?

It may seem strange that despite the agreements referred to above, a definition of dyslexia has yet to receive international consensus. One probable reason for this is that dyslexia can take so many different forms. A further reason for this lack of consensus is the debate now surrounding the neurological origins of dyslexia. Although there is agreement that there is an association between neurological factors and dyslexia, the precise way in which neurological factors are associated with dyslexia have yet to be satisfactorily established.

A further reason for the ongoing debate over dyslexia is the interesting question as to whether dyslexia should be regarded as a *different* way of learning rather than a *weakness*. Some support for this view comes from the research into the different hemispheres of the brain. It has been discovered, for instance, that the right hemisphere of the brain is often larger than the left hemisphere in dyslexic people and it is the right hemisphere that is said to be mainly concerned with visual processing. Moreover, it has been established that most dyslexic children tend to favour a more visual learning style. It is this kind of evidence that has caused some authors to question whether dyslexia is a deficit after all or simply a different way of learning.

The theory of *multiple intelligences* and the topic of *learning styles* have added further support to the view that dyslexia may simply be a different way of learning. It is evident that dyslexic people can be intelligent in ways other than linguistically. This is obvious enough when we consider the number of famous and successful people who were diagnosed as dyslexic when children. If dyslexic children tend to operate with a more visual style as has been suggested, perhaps they are being penalized by society's emphasis on linguistic skills. On the other hand, our society today is so dependent on the written word that dyslexic children would be penalized even further without developing literacy skills. I am sure that most teachers and parents would agree that no matter whether their literacy difficulties are considered to be a difference or a deficit, children with dyslexia still need to learn how to read in order to compete in today's world.

The ordinary class teacher is in the best position to be able to identify the characteristics of dyslexia in a child, as well as often being able to provide the best help. However, it would be unrealistic and probably unnecessary to expect all class teachers to undertake a special course in the teaching of dyslexic children. At the same time, there is no reason why all teachers should not be familiar with the concept of dyslexia, and learn how to support dyslexic children.

All teachers want the children in their care to do well and it is always of concern to discover that one or two children in the class are not making the expected progress. This can be distressing for a teacher when this happens, despite skilled teaching. Lack of progress in their child can also be disturbing for parents. It is especially disturbing if the child's lack of progress is in learning to read. As reading pervades the whole school curriculum, a child who is unable to read properly is going to have difficulties with other subjects as well. Fortunately, with skilled teaching, most children who have difficulty learning to read eventually do make progress. However, not all children respond that easily ... despite skilled teaching. There are many reasons why some children may not respond easily, even when given extra help. These reasons may be medical, emotional or intellectual, and sometimes all factors are responsible. One important intellectual reason for continued literacy difficulties is that some children are dyslexic. Surveys indicate that approximately 10–15 per cent of children have literacy difficulties to some degree that would be described as dyslexic.

Although teachers and parents are usually the first to identify signs of dyslexia in a child, it is not always easy to confirm dyslexia without an expert diagnosis. One important reason why an expert diagnosis is desirable is because there are other specific learning difficulties that often manifest similar characteristics as dyslexia. It is easy to confuse dyslexia with any one of these. However, once dyslexia has been confirmed, it is important that appropriate help is given as soon as possible. If appropriate help is not provided early for dyslexic children, they will not only continue to fail in schoolwork but the chances are that they may also develop behavioural problems.

Even where it is accepted that a child is failing in schoolwork and is in need of special help, some teachers and parents still find it difficult to accept that the reason for the child's difficulties may be dyslexia. One reason why they may be reluctant to accept that dyslexia is a possibility may be that many teachers and parents do not fully understand the concept. Sadly, it is not only some teachers and parents who may show a lack of awareness of the meaning of dyslexia. This state of affairs is not uncommon in society generally. One example of this is the person who thinks that dyslexia is a medical issue For parents with that view, to be told that their child has something they believe to be a medical problem can be distressing.

There have been many myths over the years surrounding the topic of dyslexia. The myth that dyslexia is a medical problem is still harboured by a surprising number of people. This reason why this myth continues is probably because there was a time when dyslexia was indeed considered to be a pathological condition. This was in the days before the accumulation of the research into the origins of dyslexia that exists today. We now know that dyslexia is not a pathological condition. There is general agreement today that although dyslexia may well have biological and neurological origins, it is primarily a specific educational difficulty.

The purpose of this book

Teachers and parents should find this book a useful source of information on dyslexia in children and also on how to manage dyslexia. It should be a valuable source of reference, not only for teachers and parents, but also for professionals who may be interested in finding out about dyslexia. It can be disturbing for some parents to discover that their child is dyslexic. Accordingly, this book should be a comfort to parents and their dyslexic children, as on reading the book they will come to see that dyslexia need not necessarily be interpreted negatively. After all, some of the most creative members of society were diagnosed as dyslexic when children and subsequently went on to fame and fortune in various fields of endeavour.

In summary, the book has three major aims. The first aim is to help teachers, parents and other interested professionals understand what is meant by dyslexia. The second aim is to show them how best to teach and to support children with dyslexia. The third aim is to provide practical and emotional support for parents, teachers and others who may have dyslexic children in their care.

The contents of each chapter of the book are summarized in the following paragraphs.

Chapter 1 begins with the more significant events in the history of dyslexia. In order to understand what is meant by dyslexia, it is helpful first to outline a brief history of the concept from its early beginnings as a medical problem up to the present time, when both medicine and psychology are seen to be making important contributions to our knowledge of dyslexia. The various terms that have been used throughout the history of the concept of dyslexia are presented in this chapter. The history of the viewpoint that dyslexia may be a difference and not a deficit is also discussed.

It is essential that teachers, as well as parents, are aware of the characteristics of dyslexia. Although the first and most obvious manifestation of dyslexia in a child is likely to be a difficulty with learning to read, the problems of dyslexia are much wider than this. The most common characteristics of this learning difficulty are discussed in Chapter 2. The multifaceted nature of dyslexia is highlighted in this chapter. Emphasis is placed on the variety and different degrees of severity of dyslexia in each child. Common behavioural reactions that can arise as a result of dyslexia are also discussed. Most frequently it would be the teacher who first identifies the dyslexic child and asks for an assessment. However, sometimes children can hide their dyslexia, especially if they are highly intelligent. In cases like that, it is often the parents who first begin to notice their children's possible dyslexia. This is why parents as well as teachers need to be aware of the common characteristics of dyslexia.

It is curious that despite a consensus over the characteristics of dyslexia, there continues to be a debate among professionals over its precise definition. There are several different definitions of dyslexia in existence. The main definitions that have been promulgated are outlined, discussed and criticized in Chapter 3. These definitions are grouped into causal, descriptive and discrepancy definitions. Possible reasons for the different definitions are also discussed. It is suggested that the different research perspectives taken are likely to be the main reason for a lack of consensus on definitions. A further possible reason for multiple definitions may have been a result of attempts to include other types of specific learning difficulty in a single definition of dyslexia. It is suggested that these other learning difficulties are defined separately from dyslexia.

It is not always easy to identify the signs of dyslexia, or in confirming it. The problem arises mainly because of the existence of other kinds of specific learning difficulty. These other specific learning difficulties not only have some similar characteristics to dyslexia but can also overlap with dyslexia. An example of such a specific learning difficulty that could be confused with dyslexia would be *attention deficit hyperactivity disorder* (ADHD). These other types of learning difficulty are defined, categorized and listed in Chapter 4. The chapter concludes with a synthesis of the different definitions of dyslexia. A new, more precise definition, combining the previously defined causal, descriptive and discrepancy definitions is presented.

Chapter 5 discusses the skills that all children need to possess in order to be able to read. Reference is made to the specific problems faced by dyslexic children in learning these skills. The significance for the dyslexic child of a teacher's particular teaching style is also discussed. Some popular teaching strategies and remedial programmes such as the Dore programme are also discussed in this chapter. Sometimes parents ask if they can help their child read at home. The response to this request is also discussed in Chapter 5 with special attention given to the roles played by most parents at home in the development of their child's language. Suggestions are made for parents to reinforce what their child has learned at school. The importance of consulting with the child's teacher before embarking on any help at home is also emphasized.

There has been voluminous research into the possible origins of dyslexia over recent years. While this has contributed immensely to our understanding of dyslexia, it is concerning that much of these research findings do not appear to have received the publicity they deserve. It would not be possible to review all the research in this book. However, the more significant research findings into the origins of dyslexia are described in Chapter 6. This research focuses on the biological, genetic and cognitive origins of dyslexia, with particular reference to the role played by the cerebellum in phonological processing and language development. The use of functional magnetic resonance imaging (fMRI) together with positron emission tomography (PET), used to investigate hemispherical asymmetry and dyslexia as well as brain functioning in the context of this research, is also described and highlighted in Chapter 6.

Chapter 6 concludes with a discussion of the notion of multiple intelligences and learning styles in relation to the viewpoint that dyslexia may be a different way of thinking and not a *deficit* of functioning.

As previously stated, ordinary class teachers are generally the first to notice common signs of dyslexia in a child, either through their experience or through the use of appropriate tests. However, it is preferable that a professional specifically qualified in this field is asked to confirm the dyslexia. Parents sometimes worry about their child being assessed for dyslexia by a specialist. Even if they are not anxious about the process itself, it is not unnatural for parents to want to know what happens in the assessment interview. Teachers also are often curious to know what happens in the assessment. Chapter 7 aims to give this information by describing the assessment interview, the tests used and the rationale behind the tests. Some of these tests are only available to professionals who have completed a special course of training. There are other tests, however, that are available to teachers without special training. Both types of test are described in this chapter. The chapter concludes with a discussion of the reasons why it is desirable that a professional qualified in the field of dyslexia should administer the assessment.

The professional who conducts the assessment usually issues an official report. As this report quotes statistical information and uses specific terminology, the interpretation of this report can sometimes present difficulties for people unused to the special terms used. Unless specifically trained and qualified in special education, the terms used and the statistics reported may be difficult to understand. Chapter 8 sets out to help teachers and parents interpret and understand a typical report following an assessment for dyslexia.

A major feature of this book is the attention paid to the relationship between dyslexia and the development of the child's self-esteem. Chapter 9 sets out to help teachers and parents appreciate the significance of the relationship between attainment and self-esteem. There is ample research evidence showing an association between self-esteem and learning. Children who demonstrate any kind of learning difficulty are at risk of developing low self-esteem. Dyslexic children's level of self-esteem is a crucial factor in their progress. When first told that they are dyslexic, children often experience initial feelings of inadequacy. These feelings can lead to low self-esteem unless handled wisely. There is also the risk of these children developing behavioural difficulties. Chapter 9 outlines suggestions to help dyslexic children avoid these negative outcomes. Strategies are outlined for both teachers and parents to use to help maintain the dyslexic child's self-esteem.

As mentioned earlier in this Introduction, it is natural that parents should experience a degree of concern when first informed that their child has a learning difficulty. To be informed that their child is dyslexic can be a particular source of stress and in rare cases, may result in acute anxiety. Conscientious teachers often experience similar feelings when they have children in their class who fail to make progress.

It is not uncommon for parents who are closely identified with their children to begin to feel inadequate themselves. In wondering how best to help their children, they may also develop low self-esteem as well as emotional stress. Chapter 10 aims to help teachers and also parents to manage possible negative emotional reactions that can ensue from having to care for a dyslexic child.

Research has shown an association between parents' self-esteem and their children's self-esteem. Specific personal characteristics in parents' self-esteem that are conducive to high self-esteem in their children have been identified and these are outlined. The relationship between psychological stress and low self-esteem is also examined Questionnaires for teachers and parents to assess their own self-esteem as well as their stress levels are included in this chapter. Suggestions and techniques for maintaining parents' and teachers' self-esteem, as well as techniques for managing stress, are also outlined in this chapter.

Chapter 11 discusses the challenges that are faced by dyslexic children, in addition to having to cope with literacy difficulties. It is not always recognized that dyslexia can present challenges in everyday living in the community as well as being manifested as a problem with literacy. For instance, as dyslexic children usually have a weakness in short-term memory, they are likely to face difficulties in all situations that demand memory skills. These situations and concerns are outlined and discussed in Chapter 11. Dyslexia as a 'hidden disability' is also discussed, showing how the challenges faced by the dyslexic child are not always appreciated by society at large. It highlights the fact that despite optimistic messages being given by the latest research, society's attitudes towards dyslexia continue to be a cause for some concern. Some of the myths regarding dyslexia are also discussed in this chapter. The chapter concludes with arguments for and against the desirability of labelling dyslexic children.

1 The history of dyslexia

Introduction

The word *dyslexia* is only one of many terms that have been used over the years to describe children with literacy difficulties. As recently as the twentieth century some authors were expressing reservations over using the word dyslexia to describe this group. Even when the word dyslexia began to come into general use, many authors continued to have reservations. For instance, for some, the word dyslexia was considered to be synonymous with the term 'specific learning difficulty' (Rutter and Yule, 1975), while for others the term 'specific developmental dyslexia' (Pumphrey, 1996) was preferred.

It was not until the publication of the government document, *The Code of Practice* (Department for Education and Employment, 1994) that dyslexia was given official recognition. Even though this official document seemed at last to be giving official recognition to the existence of dyslexia, the relevant phrase in the document continued to reflect some reluctance to accept dyslexia as distinct from other learning difficulties. The document referred to 'specific learning difficulties (for example dyslexia)'. This statement probably reflected the continued reservations held at that time by several educationalists regarding the concept of dyslexia. Prior to the issue of this document, the phrases 'specific learning difficulty' or 'specific developmental dyslexia' seemed to figure more prominently in the literature to describe this group of children. Although dyslexia is accepted today as an official category of specific learning difficulty, there is a debate continuing among some educationalists over whether any kind of label is necessary to describe this category of children with learning difficulties.

The concept of dyslexia has a short history. The term dyslexia did not come into general use until the late twentieth century. Even when it became accepted that a discrete group of children with persistent literacy difficulties existed, it was some time before the word 'dyslexia' was accepted as a word to describe them.

Prior to the 1900s the topics of childhood, child development and how children learn were still the subject of much theorizing, without the advantage of today's empirical research methods. A plethora of terms was used to describe the problem, such as *word blindness*, or *strephosymbolia*. As most children's learning difficulties were at that time considered medical problems, the words used usually originated from medicine. The medical profession played the dominant role in the area of learning difficulties during those early days.

The first educationalist to investigate individual differences in children's academic abilities was Sir Francis Galton (1869). Apart from the pioneering work of Galton, neither psychology, nor the teaching profession, was making significant contributions at that time to the study of the causes of childhood learning difficulties.

Before the twentieth century, children who had literacy difficulties were considered to have medical problems, or were constitutionally limited or poorly motivated. Just how these views could have held prominence is difficult to appreciate today in the light of subsequent knowledge of child development and how children learn. The scientific study of child development had not yet fully emerged and educational psychology was in its infancy. Research journals were few in number, so even if scientific studies had taken place, there were few avenues for the dissemination of results.

The situation today, in the twenty-first century, is radically different from those early years. The development of scientific methods has allowed investigations into learning difficulties that were not previously possible. More importantly, scientific evidence for the existence of the specific learning difficulty termed 'dyslexia' is now well established. Although it had long been accepted that there is a discrete group of children who have literacy difficulties despite appropriate learning opportunities, the use of the word 'dyslexia' to describe this group is of relatively recent origin.

The different terms that have been used over the years, together with some of the significant developments in the short history of the concept, are outlined in this chapter.

Early medical perspectives

Societal interest in people with reading difficulties probably began in 1878 with Adolph Kussmaul, a German neurologist. He had a special interest in adults with reading problems who also had neurological impairment. He noticed that several of his patients could not read properly and regularly used words in the wrong order. He introduced the term 'word blindness' to describe their difficulties. The phrase, word blindness, then began to be used regularly in the medical journals to describe adults and children who had difficulty learning to read. This phrase also conveyed the fact that these patients were neurologically impaired.

In 1887, a German opthalmologist, Rudolf Berlin, was the first to use the word 'dyslexia' in place of word blindness. However, the term of dyslexia did not come into common usage in the literature until the following century. Before then word blindness was more commonly used to describe this group of adults and children with reading problems.

The next milestone in the history of dyslexia appeared in 1891 with a report in *The Lancet* medical journal by Dr Dejerne. This report described a patient who had suffered a brain injury after having been hit on the head with a crowbar. The patient had lost several language functions, including the ability to read. A medical hypothesis then emerged that concluded that those who had difficulty reading had probably suffered a brain injury.

Following Dejerne's report in *The Lancet*, further accounts began to appear in other medical journals, also reporting patients who had suffered head injuries and subsequently lost the ability to read and, in one case the ability to speak. As a result, the view that persistent reading and language difficulties always owed their origin to particular brain dysfunctions began to be generally accepted. Dejerne's work appeared to reinforce the conclusions of Kussmaul that reading difficulties were associated with underlying neurological impairments. The fact that this conclusion was merely a hypothesis and not based on any valid research was not considered. It was generally accepted at that time that difficulties in learning were rightly the province of the medical profession. Consistent with the medical model of learning that dominated that period, children who had reading difficulties were considered to have a neurological impairment. Again, these theories were held in the days before the existence of psychology as a science. The medical view of reading difficulties continued into 1900. At that time, Dr James Hinshelwood, a Scottish eye surgeon, published an account of a patient who had reading difficulties and also a congenital defect in the brain related to eyesight. From this evidence he concluded that the cause of reading difficulties was a malfunction of eyesight as a result of a brain defect. Dr Hinshelwood's work reinforced the use of the term word blindness and this phrase persisted throughout the early twentieth century.

A plethora of terms followed in the 1900s beginning with the term strephosymbolia. This term was introduced in 1925 by Dr Orton, an American neurologist of some significance. He was probably the first to recognize that children with reading difficulties often reversed letters. This phenomenon he called strephosymbolia. He also introduced the term *developmental alexia* to describe these children with reading difficulties. There were now three different terms in existence, all used to describe this learning difficulty. The problem of children with reading difficulties continued to be in the sphere of medicine.

It was not until the mid-1930s that the term dyslexia began to more commonly appear in the literature. The word dyslexia is of Greek origin and combines 'dys', meaning an absence, and 'lexia', meaning language. So, literally, the word dyslexia means an absence of language. Learning difficulties, especially dyslexia, were now beginning to be viewed primarily as educational problems. There followed a proliferation of publications of new teaching methods to help children with dyslexia. Despite these initiatives being written by educationalists, the medical profession continued to oversee the identification and placement in special schools of children with learning difficulties. This medical initiative persisted throughout the main part of the twentieth century.

Transition from a medical to an educational perspective

It was not until the mid-twentieth century that children with specific literacy difficulties began to be no longer considered to be under the jurisdiction of medicine. Educational and psychological research began to accumulate at this time, broadening understanding and refining concepts of child development. This increased knowledge base helped to redefine the origins of childhood learning difficulties and how best to manage these difficulties. Childhood learning difficulties were now more commonly recognized as being within the province of education. Even where occasionally a child's learning difficulties were diagnosed as being of a medical origin, it was agreed that the primary management of the problem was best conducted within an educational environment.

General psychology had initially helped to broaden the perspective on childhood learning difficulties. Educational psychology was now emerging as a specific branch of general psychology, further enhancing the educational perspective on learning difficulties. The significant research into the origins of learning difficulties was beginning to be carried out in the twentieth century within an educational context.

Up to the early and late twentieth century, school medical officers had been conducting the assessment of children with learning difficulties using intelligence tests devised by psychologists. It was not until the 1970s that medicine relinquished its role in that sphere and the assignment of intelligence testing was given to the educational psychologists. It was the *Warnock Report* (1978) enquiry into children with special educational needs that stimulated the change in the role of the school medical officer. Thereafter, it became inappropriate for these medical officers to be responsible for intelligence testing and also for the administrative categorization of children with learning difficulties.

The development of specific educational programmes

Prior to the twentieth century many children with learning difficulties were often considered to be unteachable. Historically, this can be seen in the two medical classifications of children at that time as being educationally subnormal and severely subnormal. The phrase 'uneducable' was sometimes used to describe children with severe learning difficulties. They were often considered to be unable to profit from education. It was not until the beginning of the twentieth century that this situation changed. As knowledge of how children learn began to accumulate, it was recognized that children previously considered to be uneducable could in fact learn, albeit at their own pace. New teaching strategies were devised and the input of educationalists began to take a more prominent role in the management of childhood learning difficulties.

Notable in this quest for new learning strategies was the work of Anna Gillingham and Bessie Stillman (1936) who published the first teaching method devised specifically to help children with reading difficulties, including those children with dyslexia. Their approach advocated a multi-sensory method based on the analysis of language. A phonic-based visual, auditory and kinaesthetic approach to the teaching of reading provided the basis of this method. Children would be asked first to say a word aloud. Then they were shown how to write the word, then how to listen to the word and, finally, they would be asked to model the word using modelling clay. The publication of their method led eventually to the modern work on the phonological aspects of reading. This method is still in use today in schools and is perhaps better know as the Gillingham–Stillman method.

Even though educationalists were seen to be taking the initiative with methods of teaching children with learning difficulties, the topic of dyslexia was still considered mainly to be the province of the medical profession. This was exemplified by the contribution of a neurologist, Dr Orton, who collaborated with the educationalists, Gillingham and Stillman, in the publication of their teaching manual.

In 1968, a more controversial method of teaching children with learning difficulties was introduced by Doman and Delacato in the USA and began to receive international attention. Although not devised specifically for dyslexic children, it is significant in the history of dyslexia as it was based on the contemporary hypothesis that deficits in the neurology of the brain are often associated with dyslexia. As such, it was probably the forerunner of several similar teaching strategies devised for dyslexic children. Since then there have been other teaching methods published that were also based on possible neurological deficits.

The Doman–Delacato method, known as 'patterning', was based on the hypothesis that 'learning-disabled children' had missed out on some of the normal neurological developmental stages. These authors asserted that these stages are the evolutionary steps that the entire human species has gone through over the generations of human development. Failure to pass through any one of these stages in an individual would result in problems in physical mobility leading to problems in language and communication.

The Doman–Delacato treatment consisted of a series of physical exercises that included motor activities such as crawling, balancing and stretching limbs. The aim was to replicate the neurological stages of development that these children were thought to have missed. The activities were to take place daily, for seven days a week and to continue for at least 12 months. They believed that at the end of the process children achieved normal hemispherical dominance and what they termed 'full neurological organization'.

Unfortunately, this innovative approach was heavily criticized following investigations by a team of medical and health specialist research workers. These investigators were unanimous in rejecting Doman and Delacato's claims for improvements in literacy skills. The work was criticized for its lack of proper theory, unsatisfactory treatment and lack of valid research. Despite the criticisms, the authors set up the *Philadelphia Institute for the Achievement of Human Potential* and have since established branches in many countries around the world. Not unnaturally, many parents have been attracted to the programme despite its apparent lack of scientific credibility. The Doman–Delacato method not only has a place in the history of dyslexia as the forerunner of other physical exercise-based programmes for children with learning difficulties through a structured programme of physical activities, but also because of its theoretical base. Doman and Delacato's original claim that abnormalities in the cerebellum might be responsible for learning difficulties has since achieved empirical support (Nicolson and Fawcett, 1995). Further methods for helping children with learning difficulties, also based on the theory that these children had neurological deficits, have since been established by Dennison (1981) in the USA and Dore (2006) in the UK. These teaching programmes both claim that learning difficulties can be remedied through physical activities that can develop 'neural pathways' in the brain. As with Doman and Delacato, Dennison and Dore have established centres throughout the world staffed by people trained to operate their programmes. The programmes are currently expanding their influence and more details concerning them are provided in Chapter 5 of this book.

The growth of independent institutions for dyslexia support

A significant event in the history of dyslexia occurred in 1963 when the Invalid Children's Aid Association (ICAA) established the Word Blind Centre for Dyslexic Children in London. Its main aim was to provide a centre for the teaching of dyslexic children although some research was also conducted. The ICAA was one of the first institutions to conduct research into the causes of dyslexia (Naidoo, 1972). The research at the Word Blind Centre provided the stimulus for further investigations into dyslexia by others who followed. One example of this is the work of Snowling (1995) into the significance of phonological processing and dyslexia.

A much-needed publicity boost for dyslexic children occurred in 1967 with the establishment in the USA of the Orton Dyslexia Society. This organization was mainly responsible for the subsequent increase in public and political attention given to the needs of dyslexic children in the USA. The Society's influence gradually extended beyond the USA, so that in 1997 it changed its name to the more appropriate title *International Dyslexia Association*, a title it holds today.

The above private institutions were the forerunners of other institutions established specifically for the purpose of support, research and teaching of dyslexic children. Today, there are literally thousands of such institutions, including university departments, spread throughout the world. There are too many to list individually; all are concerned with promoting, catering for and investigating the needs of people with dyslexia. The *British Dyslexia Association* and *Dyslexia Action* (formerly the *Dyslexia Institute*) have been particularly prominent in the UK in their promotion of the needs of dyslexic children as well as in the training of specialist teachers.

Dyslexia as a difference rather than a deficit

Dyslexia had always been researched as a deficit with research into various cognitive weaknesses and neurological deficits. However, in the early 1980s, a new notion began to emerge that seemed to be about to revolutionize the thinking on dyslexia. This notion was that dyslexia might be a *difference* and not a *deficit* after all.

The view that dyslexia might be a different way of learning probably began with the work of Gardner (1983) with his theory of multiple intelligences. Gardner took the view that intelligence was expressed in several different ways; linguistic ability being only one of them. According to Gardner's theory, we should not expect all children to be competent in linguistic skills. Gardner's theory of multiple intelligences is discussed more fully in Chapter 6 of this book.

The work of Galaburda (1989) with adults gave further support to the view proposed by Gardner. It was while performing autopsies that Galaburda noticed that there was a superior development of the right hemisphere in those who had been diagnosed as dyslexic. The right hemisphere is the part of the brain that was said to be concerned more with creativity and visual processing. The corollary to this was that dyslexic people were likely to be more creative and to use a more visual approach to learning. As the right hemisphere often seemed to be larger than the left hemisphere in dyslexic people, Galaburda proffered the view that perhaps dyslexia was a normal variation of the development of the brain and not necessarily a disorder.

The hypothesis that dyslexia is a different way of learning and not necessarily a deficit gained further publicity at this time with authors such as Silverman (2002) and Freed (1997). Silverman and Freed demonstrated how dyslexic children made excellent progress in literacy skills with programmes specifically designed to develop the facility that began to be termed 'visual spatial thinking'.

The notion that dyslexia was a different way of learning was supported by West (1997). West proffered the view that dyslexic children were 'visual thinkers' and additionally showed unusual creativity, as had been suggested by Gardner (1983). More recently, Stahl (2002) highlighted the fact that most dyslexic children tend to use a more visual learning style.

An altogether different view of dyslexia was being taken around this time by Solity (1996). Rather than entering the debate on whether dyslexia was either a deficit or a difference, Solity took the views that children with literacy difficulties had probably been deprived of appropriate learning experiences. He suggested that it was unprofitable to consider the causes of literacy difficulties within children. The origins of their difficulties were more likely to be found outside the children, in the children's environment. According to Solity, it was children's disadvantaged social environment and paucity of language experiences that resulted in literacy difficulties. Accordingly, there did not appear to be any reason why appropriate learning experiences, with children mediating their own learning, should not remediate their problems. This view received some support from the work of Kavale and Forness (1996) who found in a meta-study of 152 students with learning difficulties that 75 per cent of them had social skill deficits. Although this was a plausible theory, it is difficult to reconcile this view of dyslexia as being solely a result of social and language deprivation when considering the conclusions of recent research into the neurology of the brain. However, the Solity research has served to remind us that whatever the origins of dyslexia, or indeed whether dyslexia is a difference or a deficit, children with learning difficulties still require expert teaching.

Current perspectives

The topic of dyslexia seems now to have come full circle from its early beginnings when dyslexia used to be regarded wholly as a medical problem. Today, the medical profession, educationalists and psychologists are all collaborating in a search for the origins and treatment of dyslexia. One example of the results of this collaboration is the research that has taken place establishing the relationship between the neurology of the brain and dyslexia.

In recent times there have been dramatic developments in the use of technology to enhance the study of dyslexia. New technology has allowed research to focus on specific parts of the brain that are activated in learning so that it is now possible to localize different brain functions and to observe the extent of their differences in activation. This development came about with the invention of functional magnetic resonance imaging (fMRI) and also the positron emission tomography (PET). These machines have provided research workers with techniques that have increased our knowledge of brain functioning in general.

In contrast to former times, most of the research into dyslexia is now being conducted within the spheres of psychology and education. It is doubtful whether the study of dyslexia will ever return to the early days when it was considered to be wholly in the sphere of medicine. Whatever the future research discoveries regarding the biological and neurological origins of dyslexia, it is almost certain that the help offered to children with dyslexia will continue to be in the educational sphere.

Summary

This chapter traced the significant milestones in the history of the concept of dyslexia from its beginnings in the nineteenth century to the present time. The concept of dyslexia used to be considered a pathological condition that was wholly within the province of the medical profession. As research progressed, other terms began to be used to describe children with specific learning difficulties. It was not until the twentieth century that the term dyslexia came into general usage. Moreover, it was not until the mid-twentieth century, with the development of educational psychology, that dyslexia began to be accepted as an educational problem. This period coincided with a rise in the development of particular educational programmes designed for the remediation of learning difficulties, including dyslexia. Also notable at this time were the rise of various private organizations dedicated to the promotion of the needs of dyslexic children. The British Dyslexia Association and Dyslexia Action in the UK have been particularly prominent, not only in promoting the needs of dyslexic children, but also in the training of teachers and assessors of dyslexic children.

Although today dyslexia is generally accepted as an official category of learning difficulty, there are some authors who continue to question its usefulness as a concept. There are also those authors who accept the term dyslexia but assert that dyslexia is not a *deficit* but rather a *difference* of learning style and so a different way of functioning. This controversial view continues to be debated.

Today, in the twenty-first century, dyslexia is officially recognized and has become a topic of research for both medicine and education. The professions of medicine and psychology are seen now collaborating in significant research into the origins and management of dyslexia. Although medicine continues to play a prominent role in this research, showing that the causes of dyslexia lie within biology and neurology, its treatment will most certainly continue to be in the field of education.

2   The characteristics of dyslexia

Introduction

Dyslexia is a word used to describe a specific learning difficulty that can affect children in a variety of different ways. Although dyslexia in children is manifested primarily through literacy difficulties, it can also affect the child's everyday living. It is not always recognized that the challenges dyslexic children face are manifested also in a much wider context than those experienced during the mastering of literacy skills.

Teachers and parents will be aware of just how the dyslexic child's difficulties often extend beyond the learning situation. Some of the problems that appear to be associated with dyslexia, such as a weakness in short-term memory and slowness to process information, may also affect other situations where quick responses are required. Parents will be familiar with problem of their child forgetting seemingly simple instructions such as remembering to brush their teeth. Teachers will be familiar with dyslexic children who always seems to need extra time to put on their coats when it is home time. Dyslexic children may also have difficulties in their social relationships and in coping with new situations outside school.

The multifaceted nature of dyslexia together with the reactions to the frustrations of dyslexia is discussed in this chapter. The chapter begins by outlining some of the problems faced in identifying the signs of dyslexia.

Confusion identifying the signs of dyslexia

Although teachers are usually the first to identify the signs of dyslexia in a child, it is sometimes easy for a teacher to miss these indicators. One reason for this oversight may be that not all children who are dyslexic show obvious signs of it. Dyslexia is especially difficult to identify if the child is intelligent, well behaved and helpful in class. Intelligent children can also learn to use various strategies to avoid their failures being exposed; in other words, children can easily learn to 'mask' their dyslexia. Conversely, some dyslexic children can give the false impression that they are of low intelligence, especially if they are introverted in temperament and shy of social contact. In these circumstances, it is not unknown for parents to be informed by teachers that their children are of limited ability when the parents firmly have evidence to the contrary. Parents usually defend their children in this instance with comments asserting that their children are 'different at home'. Many children probably are 'different' in the security of the home environment where they can more easily be themselves.

It would be easy for parents to become defensive in the face of a teacher's opposite view of their child's ability. However, it is important that this tendency is resisted and that the parents remain positive. They should discuss these conflicting impressions with the child's teacher and give reasons why they feel their child is bright. Most teachers under these circumstances would be only too ready to listen to the parents. It may be advisable also to seek an interview with the school's Special Needs Coordinator (SENCO). Parents will find often that the SENCO is the person in the school who is most experienced and knowledgeable regarding the concept of dyslexia and its management.

Another major reason why it is not always easy to notice the signs of dyslexia is that it takes many different forms. Dyslexia is a multifaceted problem. Dyslexia can so often be mistaken for other learning difficulties that manifest similar signs.

Additionally, some children may appear to have dyslexia when the causes of their problems lie in other areas than dyslexia. For example, they may have simply missed much of the early years of schooling. One example of this was the situation of an eight-year-old girl referred to the author because she was manifesting signs of dyslexia. On further investigation it was discovered that the family had moved their place of abode frequently and the child had attended six different schools. The reason for the girl's problems was that she had not stayed long enough in any one school to profit from the education provided.

⎮ A further problem in identifying possible signs of dyslexia is that all children, during the early stages of development, show some of the characteristics of dyslexia. It is only when a child is introduced to the learning of literacy skills and shows difficulties in acquiring these skills that dyslexia might be suspected⎮ This is why one would be unlikely to be able to confirm dyslexia at the preschool age. For instance, most preschool children have yet to establish lateral dominance.

Once in school many children have still not established a lateral dominance. This is why children have a tendency to reverse letters when first introduced to reading and writing. This means that many children will show some characteristics of dyslexia during the first two years of schooling without necessarily being dyslexic. The difference for the child with dyslexia is that the characteristics may present as a cluster of behavioural signs seemingly not amenable to change. These signs persist over time and continue to cause difficulties with learning. Also, children with dyslexia may often manifest them to a more severe degree.

The characteristics of dyslexia

The following list describes some of the common characteristics of dyslexia in children:

- has difficulty reciting nursery rhymes;
- cannot easily remember verbal instructions;
- is unusually slow to write and to copy;
- has trouble distinguishing left from right;
- is easily distracted;
- has a short attention span;
- often demonstrates restless behaviour;
- shows little interest in reading;
- becomes embarrassed if asked to read in public;
- demonstrates a lack of confidence in own ability;
- easily forgets a sequence of steps, for example, tying shoelaces;
- often reverses the order of words or letters when speaking;

- easily forgets the order of events, for example, days of the week;
- shows poor ability for spatial relationships, for example, gets lost easily;
- has difficulty learning the alphabet;
- confuses the order of sounds, for example, says par cark instead of car park;
- has problems with general organization, for example, tidying up bedroom;
- often appears apathetic and unable to act without instructions;
- easily forgets verbal instructions;
- is often slow to respond to oral instructions;
- is slow to copy from a board or overhead projector;
- is slow to learn arithmetical tables.

It is important to note that this list is not exhaustive and that not of all these characteristics will be present in a single dyslexic child. Moreover, any one of these characteristics could be indicative of other specific learning difficulties, as discussed in Chapter 3. In order to ensure that the manifested characteristics are representative of dyslexia and not another type of problem, it is desirable that a qualified professional conducts the assessment. However, teachers and parents are in a good position to identify signs of possible dyslexia in the first instance, even if the final confirmation of dyslexia may need to be made by a qualified professional.

Lack of lateral dominance

A common symptom of dyslexia among the above list is a problem in choosing between left and right. All children experience this confusion until they have established lateral dominance. Eventually, most children establish a dominance of eye, hand and leg. They have a natural preference to use either their left side or their right side, according to which hemisphere in the brain has developed dominance (Harris, 1979). A minority of children usually termed 'ambidextrous' appear to be comfortable using either side. Sometimes, however, there is a developmental delay in the establishment of dominance and in some instances dominance is never properly established. Children with this problem continue to have trouble selecting left from right. These are the children who often have a tendency to reverse letters such as 'b' and 'd'. They may eventually learn which is left and right and with practice will usually overcome the problem. However, there will usually be some delay when having to respond as the need to reverse things often persists. When dominance is not fully developed by the age of about seven or eight, the child is said to have lateral confusion, which may be a sign of dyslexia.

Weaknesses in working memory

There is agreement in the literature that a weakness in working memory is associated with dyslexia (Rack, 1994). Working memory is also referred to as short-term memory (Baddeley, 1986). A weakness in working memory is most commonly exemplified when children forget oral instructions. Parents of dyslexic children will probably remember their children having a problem in such instructions as requests to remember to brush their hair, wipe their shoes on the mat, and so on. Teachers will commonly find that the child with dyslexia has a problem recalling nursery rhymes and also with remembering verbal instructions. Unless teachers and parents understand this weakness in working memory, it can be frustrating for them when the child regularly forgets things.

There is often a difference between dyslexic children's rote short-term memory and their sequential memory. For example, dyslexic children may be able to repeat a series of unrelated numbers but find it difficult to remember their correct sequence when carrying out an arithmetical division sum. A difficulty with mathematics is common in dyslexic children, although not all dyslexic children have this problem. *Dyscalculia* is the term given to this problem with mathematics.

Possible weakness in visual memory

Although it is in the auditory sphere that the dyslexic child appears to have the main problem with short-term memory, there is some evidence that visual memory may also be a problem in some dyslexic children (Goulandris and Snowling, 1991). However, rather than there being this link between visual memory *per se* and dyslexia, it has been suggested that an apparent weakness in visual memory might be a symptom of a magnocellular impairment. Magnocells are neurones in the brain that are responsible for the synchronization of events. The role of the magnocells is discussed further in Chapter 6. In general, however, it would appear that dyslexic children have superior abilities in the visuo-spatial area and fewer problems in visual memory (Galaburda, 1989).

Behavioural consequences of dyslexia

Children with dyslexia may experience intense frustrations so would be at risk of developing behavioural difficulties. This is especially so if their dyslexia is not identified early and appropriate help given. The reason for this frustration is that they are continually expected to perform in areas they find difficult. The following frustration reactions are commonly observed if dyslexic children do not receive appropriate help.

Lack of confidence

A familiar consequence of consistent failure in schoolwork for many children is a general lack of confidence. Research has consistently shown a positive correlation between low self-esteem and a failure to achieve in schoolwork (Lawrence, 2006). Children with any kind of learning difficulty, including dyslexia, are always at risk of developing low self-esteem.

Children with low self-esteem achieve less and tend to demonstrate more behavioural difficulties. Low self-esteem affects not only children's ability to learn but it may also affect their performance in everyday pursuits. Without help, their failure in literacy skills tends to generalize to the whole personality, so that before long they begin to feel failures generally and lack confidence in most situations. This is why it is important that dyslexic children are identified early in their school career, before they have too many experiences of failure.

With prolonged failure, children with dyslexia will become discouraged and eventually stop trying to achieve. Their self-image is changed from perceiving themselves as children who can learn to children who fail. Eventually, they will accept this new negative self-image. If, on the other hand, their dyslexia is identified early, they will receive appropriate teaching and their self-esteem will be maintained. The topic of self-esteem and dyslexia is discussed in more detail in Chapter 9.

External locus of control/learned helplessness

Locus of control is a learned characteristic and a term used to describe the extent to which people feel responsible for their behaviour, including their academic performance. It is a term coined by Rotter (1954) and refers people's belief in their ability to control events in their life. Locus of control can be measured along a continuum with internal locus of control at one end of the continuum to external locus of control at the other end of the continuum. Most people lie in the middle of this continuum. Those people who consider their behaviour and their performance to be totally the result of factors outside of themselves are said to be *externally controlled*. Those who consider that they are totally responsible for their behaviour and their performance are said to be *internally controlled*. Clearly, extreme attitudes of both external and internal control would be unhealthy. This is because some things, such as chance events occurring, are outwith our control. It is unhealthy to believe that everything that happens to us is a result of our own efforts. On the other hand, to believe that we have no control over anything at all is unrealistic and equally unhealthy.

Dyslexic children are always at risk of developing external control. Those who do not receive help with their dyslexia become discouraged. No matter how hard they may try, they do not seem to be able to succeed. Consequently, they begin to feel that they have no control over what happens to them. Eventually they become totally accepting of their inability to succeed and become apathetic, lacking the motivation to achieve. This characteristic of external control has been term by Seligman (1991) as 'learned helplessness'.

Aggressive behaviour

A common reaction to frustration of any kind is aggression. The child with dyslexia is particularly at risk of experiencing frustration, both at school and at home. Without appropriate help, they are inevitably going to be frustrated by their inability to keep up with other children. At the very least this can make them appear 'bad-tempered', both at school and at home. At home they may be regarded by their parents as noncompliant and be inappropriately chastised. In school, they may become outwardly aggressive and are often seen fighting other children. On the other hand, they may react with 'silent aggression', that is, by refusing to attempt to cooperate. Whether aggression is manifested outwardly in an extroverted fashion or silently in an introverted fashion depends on the innate temperament of the child. The temperamentally extroverted child would be the one most likely to shout and to pick a quarrel with other children. The temperamentally more introverted child would be more likely to react by sulking or withdrawing from the scene. Strategies for coping with these problems are discussed further in Chapter 9.

Summary

Dyslexia is a multifaceted learning difficulty. The fact that there are many characteristics of dyslexia is one reason why it is sometimes difficult to identify. Moreover, most young children will show some characteristics of dyslexia during the early stages of development. An example of this is a 2 year old child who has not yet achieved lateral dominance and so is likely to use both hands interchangeably. If the same child demonstrates this behaviour at about the age of 8 years, then it may well be a sign of dyslexia. Another reason why it is sometimes difficult to identify the signs of dyslexia is that some children are able to 'mask' their dyslexia by using various strategies to avoid being seen to fail.

As dyslexia may take many forms, simply describing a child as dyslexic communicates nothing about the nature of that child's difficulties. To describe a child as 'dyslexic' merely informs that the child has a learning difficulty. In order to understand a child's dyslexia it is important to know the age of the child, how the dyslexia is being manifested and to what degree.

Although dyslexia is generally considered mainly to be a language difficulty, it is important to recognize that the problems facing the dyslexic child are much wider than this. The difficulties faced by the child with dyslexia in the learning of literacy skills may also affect their everyday living. One example of this is the dyslexic child with a weakness in short-term memory who continually forgets to carry out delegated tasks. Unless the wider aspects of dyslexia are recognized, the child will become frustrated and behavioural difficulties are likely to occur. Negative behaviour may also arise in the dyslexic child unless their dyslexia is identified early and appropriate help and support provided. These are strong arguments for all teachers and parents of dyslexic children to be sensitive to the signs of dyslexia and the needs of dyslexic children.

3 Defining dyslexia

Introduction

Although there is much agreement on the possible manifestations of dyslexia, there is no international consensus over its definition. Teachers and parents often ask, 'How common is dyslexia?' This is not an easy question to answer, because there are many different definitions of dyslexia. A variety of definitions have been used in incidence surveys and inevitably have produced different results. Consequently, we can only talk in terms of an estimated incidence of dyslexia. Despite the lack of consensus regarding the definition of dyslexia, most educationalists throughout the western world would agree that at least 10 per cent of the child population are probably dyslexic. In real terms, this means that you would expect to find one or two dyslexic children in every class in any school.

This chapter reviews the different definitions that exist and the probable reasons why defining dyslexia has been problematic. Three probable reasons for this difficulty are outlined. The first reason is due to the attempts to incorporate the multifaceted nature of dyslexia into a single definition. The different manifestations of dyslexia between children and adults most readily illustrate this problem defining dyslexia. The second reason is because of the different research perspectives taken in regard to the causes of dyslexia. The final reason is a result of trying to incorporate into a single definition other related specific learning difficulties that often overlap with dyslexia.

The chapter outlines, categorizes and critically examines current definitions of dyslexia. The chapter concludes with a suggested definition that incorporates previously defined descriptive and causal definitions with the addition of a discrepancy perspective.

The multifaceted nature of dyslexia

It has proved to be a challenge to embrace the presentation of the different characteristics of dyslexia in a single definition. Also, attempts to formulate a definition that would apply equally to adults and to children has proved to be an almost impossible task. There has been a tendency to assume that dyslexia is similar in both children and adults, when in fact there are several differences. The ways in which dyslexia is manifested in an adult compared with the ways in which it is manifested in the child are much more complex. Unlike the dyslexic child, learning to read is rarely the main problem for the adult. Most adult dyslexics have learned to read quite well even if they may continue to have problems with spelling. The adult may well show some of the problems with literacy like the dyslexic child but the adult with dyslexia has also to cope with demands in society outside school that the dyslexic child rarely encounters.

Different theoretical research perspectives

There appear to be three major theoretical research perspectives apparently impeding the formulation of a single definition of dyslexia. These perspectives can be grouped into the neurological/biological, the cognitive and the educational. They comprise both causal and descriptive definitions, each one reflecting a different field of research interest. Inevitably their conclusions have been reflected in their own definitions of dyslexia. Accordingly, the researchers themselves may have hindered the search for a consensus unwittingly. Although, without doubt, the different research perspectives taken have enhanced our general understanding of dyslexia, they may well have hindered a consensual definition. An attempt to accommodate the different research perspectives into a single definition of dyslexia continues to prove difficult.

Other specific learning difficulties overlapping with dyslexia

There are several specific learning difficulties that some authorities have attempted to incorporate into a definition of dyslexia. This would seem to have unnecessarily complicated the formulation of a single definition. It is suggested here that these other specific learning difficulties be defined separately from dyslexia. Some of these difficulties can easily be confused with dyslexia as they manifest similar behaviours and may even accompany dyslexia. They can be grouped into cognitive, sensory and behavioural problems. Examples of each would be dyscalculia, scotopic sensitivity and attention deficit hyperactivity disorder (ADHD), respectively. These other specific learning difficulties are defined and discussed in more detail in Chapter 4.

Definitions of dyslexia

As well as the variety of definitions introduced by different research workers, formal definitions of dyslexia have been introduced by special interest groups such as the *British Dyslexia Association*, the *British Psychological Society, Dyslexia Action* and the *International Dyslexia Association*. An analysis of these definitions that have been generated by interest groups can be divided into the two major categories of causal and descriptive definitions. These are explained as follows.

Causal definitions

This type of definition has emerged from the research into the neurological and biological causes of dyslexia. Causal definitions have been concerned with the differences in brain functioning displayed by dyslexics. They are concerned with apparent deficits in the ways in which some people interpret and process information that comes in through the senses. The focus in this type of definition has been on the inclusion of abnormalities and deficits in brain functioning. This has been achieved using the functional magnetic resonance imaging (fMRI) technique in which the activated parts of the brain can be identified. The research into a genetic basis for dyslexia would also come into this category.

Descriptive definitions of dyslexia

This type of definition is concerned with the manifestations of dyslexia. These definitions have focused on difficulties with the processes of writing, reading, spelling and general organization of everyday tasks. The description of weaknesses in levels of cognitive functioning such as phonological processing would come under this category and would also include the problems of working memory as displayed by dyslexics. A more detailed review of the research findings illustrating the different perspectives on dyslexia is presented in Chapter 6.

The main definitions that have been postulated over the years are outlined in this section. A critique is made for each definition generated by committees and individual professionals. The critique demonstrates how different research perspectives are reflected in the various definitions of dyslexia.

The World Federation of Neurology (1968)

This definition was one of the first to include both causal and descriptive perspectives.

> Dyslexia is a disorder in children who, despite conventional classroom teaching experience, fail to attain the language skills of reading, writing and spelling commensurate with their intellectual abilities.

The word *disorder* implies a medical abnormality, which is clearly considered by the authors of this definition to be the cause of dyslexia. The definition also includes a descriptive type of definition when referring to educational attainments.

The International Dyslexia Association

This definition is a further example of one that incorporated both causal and descriptive aspects. It also takes the view that dyslexia is caused by a neurological abnormality. It is perhaps more inclusive of the signs of dyslexia than the previous definitions. However, this definition would not appropriately describe the adult with dyslexia.

> Dyslexia is a specific learning disability that is neurological in origin, often familial. It is characterised by difficulties with accurate and/or fluent word recognition and by poor spelling and decoding abilities. These difficulties typically result from a deficit in the phonological component of language that is

often unexpected in relation to other cognitive abilities and the provision of effective classroom instruction. Secondary consequences may include problems in reading comprehension and reduced reading experience can impede growth of vocabulary and background knowledge.

British Dyslexia Association

This is the first definition to recognize that dyslexia may produce strengths as well as weaknesses. It is a *descriptive* definition of dyslexia. It does not attempt include possible neurological or biological causes of dyslexia.

> Dyslexia is best described as a combination of abilities and difficulties that affect the learning process in one or more of reading, spelling, writing. Accompanying weaknesses may be identified in areas of speed of processing, short-term memory, sequencing and organisation, auditory and/or visual perception, spoken language and motor skills. It is particularly related to mastering and using written language, which may include alphabetic, numeric and musical notation. Some dyslexics have outstanding creative skills. Others have strong oral skills. Some have no outstanding talents. They all have strengths. Dyslexia can occur despite normal intellectual ability and teaching. It is independent of socioeconomic or language background.

This definition makes no reference to the more complex difficulties faced by the adult as opposed to the child with dyslexia. Also, as it stands, it could apply equally to people with a general learning difficulty. It is not clear that this definition refers to a specific learning difficulty.

Dyslexia Action (formerly the British Dyslexia Institute)

This definition of dyslexia encompasses both causal and descriptive definitions and is inclusive of most of the difficulties faced by a dyslexic child.

> Dyslexia causes difficulties in learning to read, write and spell. Short-term memory, mathematics, concentration, personal

organisation and sequencing may also be affected. Dyslexia usually arises from a weakness in the processing of language-based information. Biological in origin, it tends to run in families, but environmental factors also contribute. Dyslexia can occur at any level of intellectual ability. It is not the result of poor motivation, emotional disturbance, sensory impairment or lack of opportunities, but it may occur alongside any of these. The effects of dyslexia can be largely overcome by skilled specialist teaching and the use of compensatory strategies.

As with the previous definition, it is an optimistic definition, recognizing that dyslexics often have strengths as well as weaknesses. However, this definition appears to be over-optimistic, especially when considering adults with dyslexia. The basis of this statement is the belief that dyslexia can be overcome. It is agreed that compensatory strategies can help but from available evidence it seems that most dyslexics will always have weaknesses in short-term memory that can continue to affect their lives in general.

British Psychological Society

This is a wholly descriptive definition and notable for its brevity. It may be deliberately brief with the purpose of providing a practical definition that avoids reference to possible causes of dyslexia.

Dyslexia is evident when accurate and fluent word reading and/or spelling develops very incompletely or with great difficulty.

This definition is purposely narrow and although it may well have its uses when applied to children, it most certainly does not adequately define the problem faced by adults. Moreover, as with the British Dyslexia Association's definition, it does not distinguish between children with a general learning difficulty as opposed to those with a specific learning difficulty. However, as a descriptive definition of dyslexia, it avoids the controversy over the origins of dyslexia and offers a positive view of dyslexia with a focus on the remediation of the child's difficulties.

Individual professionals

McLoughlin et al. (2002) provide a further example of a definition that comprises both causal and descriptive aspects of the problem.

> Developmental dyslexia is a genetically inherited and neurologically determined inefficiency in working memory, the information processing system fundamental to performance in conventional educational and work settings. It has a particular impact on verbal and on written communication as well as on organisation, planning and adaptation to change.

This definition is probably the most accurate and concise definition of dyslexia to date. It describes the difficulties experienced as being underpinned by a weakness in working memory. It also includes possible neurological and genetic determinants. It also accurately refers to the manifestations of the problem, measured in literacy performance. Finally, it is a definition that could be usefully applied to both children and adults. The only criticism of this definition is that it would not distinguish between those with a general learning difficulty and those with a specific learning difficulty.

The critique

There are two main criticisms that can be applied to all the above definitions of dyslexia. First, apart from the McLoughlin et al. (2002) definition, they all clearly refer to dyslexia as a childhood condition with no reference to adult dyslexia. The fact that the challenges faced by adults with dyslexia are more complex than those faced by children is ignored in these other definitions. As emphasized by McLoughlin et al. (2002), dyslexia in the adult is rarely manifested solely by literacy difficulties. As stated earlier, the problems faced by the adult with dyslexia are much more complex than those of children. Although dyslexia in a child is manifested mainly by difficulties in learning the basic literacy skills, dyslexia in the adult presents challenges to the individual also in the wider social world. The adult dyslexic has to display competence not only in literacy skills but also in the areas of finance, employment and communication. Although dyslexia in children is also manifested in their general environment outside school, children are not usually subjected to the same environmental pressures as adults.

It is claimed in this book that an accurate definition of dyslexia should comprise not only causal and descriptive perspectives but also a third one, namely, a discrepancy perspective. The discrepancy referred to is the presence of a significant discrepancy between working memory and reasoning ability in either verbal or non-verbal spheres. Reasons for including memory and reasoning ability in a definition of dyslexia are presented below. Before presenting the definition, working memory and the significance of a discrepancy between working memory and reasoning ability are explained.

Defining working memory

Working memory refers to the processing of images, events and ideas transmitted through the five senses. The concept of the human memory is one of the most highly researched and complex areas of investigation in the field of psychology (Baddeley, 1986). There are many models postulated to explain different kinds of memory. However, the primary division of memory is into short- and long-term memory. Each involves the storing of information from all the senses. Memory traces from the senses can be brought into consciousness without doing anything with it. However, when short-term memory is activated and is involved in processing information, it is referred to as 'working memory'.

An example of working memory would be the process involved when engaged in mental arithmetic. The successful completion of a mental arithmetic problem involves several intellectual tasks. It is necessary to be able to record the information through the auditory receptors, to understand the information, to retain the information, to manipulate the information and finally to verbally express the answer. Both auditory short-term memory and intelligence are involved when completing a mental arithmetic problem. This is why an assessment of mental arithmetic ability is a useful part of an assessment for possible dyslexia.

Weakness in working memory in a definition of dyslexia

There is ample research evidence suggesting an association between working memory and dyslexia that would support the inclusion of a weakness in working memory as part of a definition of dyslexia. Perfetti (1985) found that tests of working memory in young children were predictive of their future reading ability. Nicolson et al. (1992) found a deficit among dyslexics in the part of the cerebellum that involves working memory. Stanovich et al. (1997) found that children with phonological difficulties had more working memory deficits than a matched group without phonological difficulties. Finally, Rack (1994) refers to inefficiency in short-term memory as a frequent characteristic of dyslexia.

Most definitions of dyslexia recognize that a weakness in working memory is a common characteristic of dyslexia. This holds true even if authors have sometimes differed in the prominence that they have given to the weakness in working memory in arriving at a definition of dyslexia. So it would not be unreasonable to include a weakness in working memory in a definition of dyslexia.

The inclusion of a discrepancy between working memory and reasoning ability in a definition of dyslexia is further supported in a study by the author, soon to be published. This work consisted of an analysis of the test results from a sample of 447 students in further and higher education. This sample of students had been referred over an eight-year period for testing for possible dyslexia. The majority of these referrals were made following various college screening procedures that had shown the students had difficulties with academic work. Subsequent testing on the *Wechsler Intelligence Scales* revealed that 94.6 per cent of the students assessed as having a significant discrepancy between scores on subtests measuring working memory and scores on subtests tests measuring reasoning ability in either verbal or non-verbal spheres. The remaining 5.4 per cent were seen to have other reasons for their learning difficulties. These other difficulties included lack of ability, motivational factors, scotopic sensitivity or emotional problems.

Discrepancy definitions of dyslexia

Since the work of Stanovich and Stanovich (1997), arguments for the inclusion of intelligence in a definition of dyslexia have been shown to be invalid. Stanovich rightly showed that there was no correlation between a reading disability and a child's measured intelligence. As recognized by Miles and Miles (1999), children at any level of intelligence could have a specific learning difficulty. As a result of this kind of research evidence, discrepancy definitions of dyslexia have been discredited. However, there would appear to be grounds for the inclusion of a different discrepancy in a definition of dyslexia. It is suggested here that a definition of dyslexia should include a discrepancy between reasoning ability in either the verbal or the non-verbal spheres and working memory.

Tests of reasoning ability and working memory often form part of a test of global intelligence. Measures on these subtests would be important in deciding whether a child with literacy difficulties would be considered to be dyslexic or simply had a general learning difficulty. There would need to be a discrepancy between working memory and reasoning ability for the child to be considered as possibly dyslexic. If the child with literacy difficulties had a weakness in both reasoning ability and working memory, then it would be more likely that the child had a general learning difficulty. In this case, there would probably be deficits also in other areas of mental functioning, so the term 'dyslexia' would not be applied.

A new definition of dyslexia

A new definition of dyslexia is proposed in this book. It incorporates aspects of other existing definitions, especially that proposed by McLoughlin et al. (1994) but with the addition of a significant discrepancy between working memory, reasoning ability and the speed of processing information.

The task of obtaining a consensus on a definition of dyslexia has often been made difficult by the existence of other related conditions such as dyscalculia, scotopic sensitivity syndrome, dyspraxia, and so on that are often subsumed under the umbrella of dyslexia. However, to be accurate and also to be useful, it is suggested that a definition of dyslexia should exclude these other related conditions. The definition of dyslexia suggested here does not include these other specific learning difficulties.

In the light of the foregoing research and the various theories of dyslexia that have emerged, the following definition of dyslexia is suggested. This definition incorporates causal, descriptive and discrepancy theoretical perspectives.

Dyslexia is a specific learning difficulty of neurological and biological origin that is most often characterized by a significant discrepancy between measures of working memory and reasoning ability together with a weakness in the speed of processing information that may be manifested through weaknesses in a variety of educational attainments, particularly in literacy skills, as well as in everyday tasks.

There are five significant features in this definition that meet the criticisms that prevented previous definitions from gaining universal acceptance.

- Causal, descriptive and discrepancy definitions of dyslexia are included.
- It is based on significant research findings.
- The different theoretical research perspectives are reflected.
- It reconciles previous definitions of dyslexia.
- This definition would apply equally to children and to adults.
- It recognizes that children at any level of cognitive ability may have dyslexia.

In conclusion, despite a lack of consensus over how best to define dyslexia, there is universal agreement that there is an identifiable group of people who experience specific learning difficulties in the development and expression of literacy and language skills. Although the most outstanding characteristic of this group is probably their difficulty with linguistic skills, they also tend to have problems in general organization and may also have problems in social spheres. There is agreement that their difficulties appear to be inherited and associated with neurological deficits. It is agreed that dyslexic people usually demonstrate a weakness in working memory. Finally, there is agreement that the term dyslexia should be used to describe this group.

Finally, as further research takes place and our knowledge of dyslexia increases, it is possible that a future definition of dyslexia may also need to include reference to dyslexia as a difference and not as a weakness.

Summary

There is still no international consensus on a definition of dyslexia. There are three possible reasons for this lack of agreement. The first most likely reason is the multidimensional nature of dyslexia. The second possible reason is the different research perspectives adopted. Finally, the third reason for this lack of a consensus would seem to be the attempts to incorporate other types of specific learning difficulties into a single definition.

The popular existing definitions of dyslexia can be grouped under causal and descriptive definitions. However, each one of these definitions can be criticized on both theoretical and practical grounds. Accordingly, a new definition of dyslexia is proposed in this book. This new definition is suggested after consideration of the current research as well as a critique of the popular current definitions of dyslexia. This new definition would incorporate discrepancy, causative and descriptive factors and be applicable to both children and adults. It is recognized that this definition may need to be modified in the light of future research to take into account the notion that dyslexia may be a difference of functioning and not a weakness.

4 Dyslexia and other specific learning difficulties

Introduction

The characteristics of dyslexia have much in common with several other kinds of learning difficulty. This is why dyslexia can sometimes be confused with other types of problem. For instance, children with many other kinds of learning difficulty manifest a weakness in working memory and often have a short attention span, just like many dyslexic children. Although sometimes there is an overlap, there are several important differences between other learning difficulties and dyslexia. Therefore, it is not surprising if occasionally a child is referred for a dyslexia assessment and is subsequently discovered not to have dyslexia.

This chapter outlines the other most common specific learning difficulties that can be confused with dyslexia. It is advocated that these other difficulties should be defined separately. The chapter begins by contrasting a specific learning difficulty with a general learning difficulty.

General and specific learning difficulties contrasted

A general learning difficulty is manifested by weaknesses in most areas of intellectual functioning. Test scores perhaps best illustrate the difference between general and specific learning difficulties. The child with a general learning difficulty would roughly score below-average test results on all intellectual abilities tested. This would be in contrast to the test results obtained in the case of a child with a specific learning difficulty like dyslexia where there would be a wide variety of test results. For instance, most test scores may be average or above average, with below-average test scores obtained in a specific area of ability.

Specific learning difficulties can be grouped under the three headings of cognitive difficulties, sensory difficulties and physical difficulties. Although these other learning difficulties can be categorized in this way, the categories are not mutually exclusive. Many of these learning difficulties overlap one another and also may sometimes overlap dyslexia. The other types of learning difficulty that can be confused with dyslexia are discussed below.

Cognitive difficulties

Dyscalculia as part of dyslexia

'Dyscalculia' is a term that is used to describe a specific learning difficulty whereby children have problems with mathematics. There is some evidence that this kind of difficulty may be inherited (Shalev et al. 2001). Dyscalculia may or may not be part of dyslexia.

It can be appreciated why dyscalculia often accompanies dyslexia if we consider the abilities required to be able to do mathematics. Many of these functions are the same as those involved in the development of literacy skills. For instance, both learning to read and learning how to do mathematics depend on working memory and the ability to process information. This applies whether the information is presented orally or in written form. To be able to perform both these skills it is essential to be able to hold the auditory symbols in short-term memory. It is then necessary to be able to process this information or, in other words, to be able to make this information meaningful. The information then needs to be expressed either in written form or orally. This is most easily illustrated when attempting to solve a mental arithmetic problem (Chinn and Ashcroft, 1997).

A weakness in auditory sequential memory would be a handicap to successfully completing mental arithmetic problems. This is why one of the tests used in the assessment of dyslexia comprises a series of mental arithmetic problems. The information is given orally and then has not only to be retained but also to be processed. This ability is similar to that required when students have to take down notes in a lesson.

A further illustration of dyscalculia accompanying dyslexia would be working with equations in algebra. Again, a weakness in visual sequential memory would be a handicap. Algebra requires the ability to hold a series of numbers and symbols in the short-term memory, while at the same time considering a second series of numbers. This would be even more difficult for the child with dyslexia who often also has lateral confusion. A basic skill in the solving of mathematical equations is being able separate left from right (Henderson, 2000). The initial learning of multiplication tables is a further example of how a child with dyslexia is likely also to have difficulties with mathematics.

Geometry is often difficult for children with dyslexia. This is because children with dyslexia sometimes have a difficulty in organizing their visual field, as in map reading, for example. As with algebra, this subject is particularly difficult for those with lateral confusion and/or a weak visual memory.

Although a common characteristic of dyslexia is a weakness in mathematics, dyscalculia is not always present in a child with dyslexia. The reasons for this apparent anomaly are not altogether clear but it seems that some children with dyslexia have an isolated skill in mathematics.

Dyscalculia without dyslexia

Not all those who have a problem with mathematics will have dyslexia. Some children have a good working memory, are at least of average intelligence, have strong language skills but still cannot easily understand the necessary concepts involved in mathematics (Kosk, 1974). These children find it difficult to appreciate how numbers relate to one another. It also seems that they have a problem with the conception of size. They can usually learn the basic mathematical processes and arrive at the correct answers to simple mathematical problems but they often do so without really understanding the processes. They are not able to extend their mathematical abilities beyond the basic skills. The reasons for this are unclear but it is significant that the problem appears to be unrelated to levels of intelligence. Research is currently investigating the origins of this difficulty.

There is another group that manifests difficulties with mathematics but who have neither dyscalculia nor dyslexia. A detailed investigation of their problem often reveals that they have simply missed learning the basic mathematical processes. As a result they have come to believe, usually wrongly, that they would never be able to complete mathematical problems. Their main problem then becomes an emotional one. With appropriate remedial teaching and with confidence-building, this group usually makes good progress.

Attention deficit hyperactivity disorder (ADHD)

There is another condition often confused with dyslexia that is known as ADHD. This condition is manifested by problems of personality and behaviour. Children with ADHD usually have a problem with prolonged concentration, accompanied by hyperactive motor activity. It can easily be confused with dyslexia as many of the signs of ADHD are similar to those manifested by dyslexia.

There appear to be two very different views of the origins of ADHD itself. While most professionals would recognize that there is an identifiable group who demonstrate the behaviours known as ADHD, explanations for it are different. Moreover, the explanations tend to lie at different ends of a spectrum. There are those at one end of the spectrum who assert that this is a medical condition requiring medication. At the other end of the spectrum, there are those who assert that ADHD is a non-medical condition that is best managed through behavioural methods (Goodman and Poillion, 1992).

While the arguments continue, what is beyond doubt is that children diagnosed with ADHD demonstrate behaviour similar to those children diagnosed as dyslexic. As with dyslexia, a common characteristic of ADHD is a short attention span accompanied by an apparent weakness in short-term memory. Both groups of children are usually slow to develop literacy skills, but while the main reason for this in the dyslexic child is usually slowness to develop phonological skills, the main reason in those with ADHD is that they find concentration a problem. Both the child with ADHD and the dyslexic child may show hyperactive behaviour. However, the origins of this behaviour are different in each case. Whereas the restless behaviour seen in the child with ADHD is thought to be constitutional in origin, this kind of behaviour in the child with dyslexia is more likely to be a reaction to frustration.

Unless identified early, children who have dyslexia will eventually show many of the signs commonly seen in children with ADHD. Their frustration at not being able to achieve the skills required can cause them to become not only restless, but also to demonstrate behavioural problems. Both groups are prone to extreme hyperactive behaviour if their problems are not identified and treated early. Clearly they each require different kinds of treatment. (See Appendix III for a screening checklist for ADHD.)

Autism and Asperger's syndrome

As with ADHD, autism and Asperger's syndrome are mainly characterized by personality and behavioural problems. In these cases, however, it is the child's difficulties with communication that may sometimes be confused with dyslexia. The main difference between autism and Asperger's syndrome is that children with Asperger's syndrome usually have well-developed language skills while those with autism usually have a language difficulty. Autism and Asperger's syndrome range along a continuum from being mild to severe, which is why the condition is often referred to as the *autistic spectrum* (Wing, 2001).

Children with both of these syndromes typically appear to be aloof and unable to empathize with other people or to interpret other people's feelings. For example, they tend to react literally to instructions so are unable to appreciate absurdities in another person's speech. They are likely to play unimaginatively. They are particularly lacking in the ability to pick up non-verbal cues so will tend to behave in a socially inept fashion. In the same way as they are unable to appreciate that other people have feelings, they themselves appear to be unable to express emotions. These syndromes are often accompanied by fine and gross motor coordination difficulties. As well as sometimes being confused with dyslexia, the condition of these children can also be confused with ADHD.

There can be a genuine overlap between dyslexia and these syndromes. For instance, people with Asperger's and also those with autism tend to have difficulty making academic progress, despite sometimes having a high level of intelligence. They will work at their own pace and often be oblivious of time demands. Accordingly, similarly to those with dyslexia, they will show frustration if demands are made on them to complete a task in an allotted time. Many Asperger's children lack motivation to perform, so they often lack concentration and give up easily on academic tasks.

It can be appreciated how the child with autism or Asperger's syndrome can be confused with the child who has dyslexia when so many of their behaviours may be similar. The situation is made more difficult by the fact that both are likely to produce a false positive result on a screening test for dyslexia. This is why, once again, it is only through a detailed assessment that the condition can be identified as a personality problem rather than a cognitive difficulty.

Sensory difficulties

Irlen syndrome or scotopic sensitivity

There is an identifiable group who have a problem with the physical effort of reading but who in other circumstances have normal vision. They may experience a variety of problems when reading, such as distortions of print, apparent movement of print, problems with visual tracking and experiencing unusual glare from a page of writing. Olive Meares (1980), a teacher in New Zealand, was probably the first to notice these problems. She also noted that the reading of these children is sometimes characterized by having to place their finger beneath each line to prevent them from losing their place on the paper. This problem is said to originate from sensitivity to particular light frequencies and is not related to visual refractive errors. Although children with this condition are able to read and write, the effort that they put into these activities eventually can result in serious fatigue, thus slowing their performance.

Today, the terms scotopic sensitivity syndrome or Irlen sydrome, named after Helen Irlen (1991) are more commonly used to describe children who have this condition. Helen Irlen, in the USA, while researching adults with reading difficulties, also noted perceptual problems and was the first to catagorize the vast array of perceptual distortions that can occur. Irlen then went on to devise a method for testing and helping children with this problem using coloured overlays and tinted spectacles. After spending the first five years exclusively researching the method with adults, Irlen's research was expanded to include both children and adults.

In the past, the successful treatment for the Irlen syndrome was questioned as being a result of the placebo effect in both adults and children. That is, any different treatment will produce a temporary improvement simply by virtue of its novelty. However, long-term studies resulting in a strong body of evidence appears to have substantiated the benefits of using Irlen-coloured lenses or coloured overlays

(Wilkins, 1995). There are now over 60 research studies documenting positive changes in reading rate, accuracy, comfort and comprehension following the prescription of coloured lenses. Sufferers with this condition claim relief as well as increased speed of reading, improved comprehension, ability to read longer and with less strain upon using coloured overlays (Evans, 2001; Smith and Wilkins, 2007). The prescription of the filters and also the prescription of coloured lenses became a major commercial venture for many early researchers into this syndrome. The Irlen Institute in California is known worldwide not only for its commercial ventures but also for the spread of Irlen Centres in most parts of the English-speaking world. They are not only involved in assessing for the syndrome but also for conducting valuable research into it. They have also instituted a training programme for future assessors of the condition.

Although teachers are often the first to notice signs of possible scotopic sensitivity in a child, symptoms of this condition are often noticed for the first time during an assessment for dyslexia. Children being tested may, for instance, screw up their eyes when reading or show visual discomfort when having to complete visual tasks and may complain that their eyes are tired and need resting. If children experience these symptoms and their visual acuity is known to be normal, it would be advisable for the tester to obtain the skills of a trained practitioner for a fuller investigation into possible Irlen syndrome. Most educational psychologists will not be trained in this area of work. There are several questionnaires available for the purpose of screening for possible scotopic sensitivity. One of these questionnaires is presented in Appendix I as an illustration.

Binocular instability

Some children appear to have eye movements when reading that tend to want to go from right to left. This will produce obvious problems when reading as reading for comprehension requires eye movements in the opposite direction. Children with this problem are slower than most to read and find that they cannot easily fixate on words and letters (Garzia, 1993). The problem is often further exacerbated by the fact that many dyslexics have lateral confusion and have a natural tendency to reverse letters and words. However, while binocular instability slows down the reading process, it is difficult to regard this difficulty as an aspect of dyslexia as defined.

It has also been suggested that a deficit in the magnocells in the brain that control both the timing of visual and motor events could cause a problem with the synchronization of events such as visual tracking. In a study by Borsting (1996), 75 per cent of poor readers had defects in the magnocellular pathways of the midbrain. A defect in this region of the brain would result in visual information being slowed down *en route* to the cortex. Eye movements would not be synchronized with the perceived visual input. This may be one explanation why dyslexic children are often slow to read as well as having a tendency to confuse the order of words and letters.

Physical difficulties

Dyspraxia and dysgraphia

Dyspraxia is a term sometimes used to describe children who have a motor coordination weakness. It used to be known as the 'clumsy child syndrome'. Dyspraxia is manifested by coordination problems in acts such as balancing, walking, kicking a ball and catching a ball. It is known that the cerebellum part of the brain controls movement so it is hypothesized that children with dyspraxia have a weakness in this part of the brain. Although difficulties in gross motor coordination among dyslexic children are not uncommon, not all children identified as being dyslexic have dyspraxia. Conversely, those who show motor coordination problems do not always have learning difficulties.

Fine motor coordination problems are sometimes found in dyslexic children. Their handwriting is often illegible and the term 'dysgraphia' is used to define this difficulty. It is significant, however, that many children with these problems do not necessarily show learning difficulties.

In view of the established link between the cerebellum and motor coordination, some workers have developed physical programmes and exercises to improve motor coordination, claiming that this in turn has an effect on literacy skills. The hypothesis is that the various exercises and activities in these programmes integrate other brain functions, including the language areas of the brain. These exercise programmes are discussed further in Chapter 6.

In conclusion, the existence of other specific learning difficulties that can be confused with dyslexia reinforces the need for children to have a detailed assessment by a qualified professional in order to confirm the precise nature of their learning difficulties.

Summary

There are several types of specific learning difficulty that can easily be confused with dyslexia. These types of learning difficulty appear to fall into the three categories of cognitive weaknesses, sensory or physical problems and problems of personality. Each of these specific learning difficulties is often characterized with similar behaviour to children with dyslexia. Moreover, they sometimes accompany dyslexia and can overlap with it. There have been attempts to incorporate some of them into a single definition of dyslexia. As discussed in the previous chapter, this may have been one reason why there is still no consensus on a definition of dyslexia. In the interests of clarity and accurate assessment of a learning difficulty, it is suggested that other learning difficulties are considered separately from dyslexia. The existence of these, often similar specific learning difficulties, lends further support for the need for a detailed psychological assessment by either a psychologist or a specialist teacher.

5 Teaching the dyslexic child

Introduction

The question is sometimes asked, 'Is there is a cure for dyslexia?' As dyslexia is primarily a learning difficulty, and not a medical condition like a fever, it is not particularly useful to think in terms of a cure. A more appropriate question would be, 'Will my child with dyslexia eventually learn to read?' The answer to this is a definite 'Yes'.

This chapter aims to help teachers and parents understand the complex process of how children learn to read, with particular reference to the challenges faced by dyslexic children in this process. Before children are able to profit from reading instruction and so are able to read for meaning, there are basic skills that they need to have learned. These skills are described in this chapter, together with suggestions for teachers and parents on how best to help children develop them. The need for parents to collaborate with the child's teacher when doing this is emphasized.

Language development and its relation to reading readiness are explained. The strategies parents might employ in helping to develop children's language are also described. Popular methods of teaching reading and the teacher's particular learning style in this process are also discussed in this chapter. Two popular remediation programmes based on possible cerebella deficits are also discussed. The chapter begins with an account of the basic pre-reading skills that all children need to possess before they are able to progress to formal reading.

Developing the basic skills required

There are several basic skills that children have to learn before they are ready to profit from formal reading instruction. There is little point therefore in expecting children to begin to learn to read until they have learned these skills.

Reading consists of a series of quite complicated sub-skills and could be defined as the interpretation of the symbols that we call letters and words, together with their comprehension. The reading process demands skills in both auditory and visual perception as well as an adequate language facility. Most dyslexic children have had a problem with learning these skills. It is important that teachers of young children identify the children who do have this problem as there is evidence that those who have difficulties in learning pre-reading skills are those who subsequently go on to have difficulties in reading (Blachman, 1997). The ways in which dyslexia is manifested and its causes may be different in each child but there are some difficulties that are generally shared by all dyslexic children. These difficulties lie in the spheres of speech, language and the ability to learn phonological skills (Johnston, 1998). The sub-skills that make up phonological processing are described below.

Recognizing letters

A child has to perceive the different shapes made by letters before recognizing the whole word. Teachers normally would adopt a multisensory approach for children in the learning of these skills. This means that the child's visual, auditory and kinaesethic senses are all employed. For instance, the child would be asked to say the letter, then write the letter and then perhaps be asked to trace the letter. These activities are often supplemented by other tasks such as drawing around shapes and colouring them. Most children develop their visual discrimination skill with this method. For dyslexic children, the multi-sensory approach is an essential method of learning (Mortimore, 2003).

If the child is not ready, or is unable, to perform these tasks, the teacher might help the child explore the three-dimensional shape of a letter in plastic or wood. A task involving the matching of a selection of different shapes is another favourite activity designed to develop the skill of visual discrimination.

Letter orientation

Young children soon learn that toys such as a doll or a chair are still called a doll or a chair no matter whether they are presented upside down or facing different ways. However, when learning the names of individual letters they have to learn that orientation is important. For instance, they have to learn that a 'b' becomes a 'd' when it is facing the other way. All children need to learn this skill but dyslexic children are usually slow to acquire it, which is why reversals are so common among those with dyslexia.

The alphabet

The child has to learn not only the 26 letters of the alphabet but also the 17 capital letters that are different from their lower-case forms. It is not necessary for them to learn the actual sequence of the letters of the alphabet during the early years of learning to read. The ability to be able to do this develops later. Dyslexic children often have difficulty with learning the correct sequence of things in general, so the learning of the alphabet can be a slow process and should not be hurried.

Learning phonemes

The ability to read also depends on being able to distinguish between different letter sounds as well as their shape. The child has to understand that the 'squiggles' adults call words are made up of sounds. The letter sounds are called *phonemes*. Before being able to learn this skill the child must first be able to distinguish different sounds in everyday speech. The learning of this skill is often difficult for dyslexic children, but before suspecting dyslexia there is another important question that must be asked, 'How well does the child hear?' It is important to know that the child does not have a hearing problem.

It might be thought that the easiest way to teach auditory discrimination skills is merely to sound out each letter and help the child associate the sound with the shape of the letter. For most children, however, this kind of activity can be boring. A far more attractive and more motivating way to teach the letter-sound associations is through nursery rhymes. Another favourite activity is to get children to sort pictures of common objects into groups according to the initial sound of each object. This activity could be supplemented and perhaps made more motivating by introducing previously tape-recorded sounds. The old 'I-Spy' game is also a favourite activity that achieves this goal.

Learning digraphs

The child has eventually to learn the sounds of different combinations of letters. These are called *digraphs*. Most combinations comprise two letter combinations although eventually there will be larger groups of letters to be learned, such as 'ough'. It is not only dyslexic children who have difficulty with learning this skill. In the early stages of learning to read, many children have a problem remembering the different combinations, as there are so many different permutations of these sounds. This is why learning the English language is not always easy for people whose first language is not English. At this stage the child might be introduced to some regular rules regarding the reading process. One example is the blending of consonants and then showing how some blends occur together frequently while others never occur together. Examples of this would be the letters 'f' and 'r' that are often seen together (fr) whereas the letters 'f' and 'g' (fg) are never together. The imaginative teacher will devise games to teach these blends.

Identification of possible dyslexia while teaching

It is during the learning of these pre-reading skills that teachers often observe dyslexia for the first time in children. Those likely to be dyslexic are seen to be struggling with the pre-reading activities, with phonological analysis in particular, and perhaps also with the development of left to right orientation. Many young children initially have some difficulty learning these pre-reading skills. However, the child with dyslexia continues to struggle with learning them long after the others have mastered the skills. The observant teacher will soon identify the child with possible dyslexia as they are seen to be struggling with the learning of these skills. The teacher will have noticed also that as time goes on the dyslexic child's attitude towards the learning of these skills will no longer be as positive. Unless the difficulties experienced by the dyslexic child are identified early, the child is likely to become more frustrated and eventually may develop behavioural difficulties and may be reluctant to go to school.

Reading schemes

Once children have learned the above pre-reading skills, they are usually introduced to more formal reading materials. What kinds of reading material are chosen depends usually on the particular method of teaching reading favoured by the teacher. The quest for the 'best' method of teaching children to read has occupied educationalists for decades.

Many different methods of teaching reading have been introduced over the years; each being a favourite method for teachers at different times. There have been those who have strongly advocated what became known as the 'look and say' approach where children were shown the picture of the word to be learned alongside the written word. Then there is the 'phonic' approach, with emphasis on teaching reading through learning the letter–sound associations. This is fine with most children although the dyslexic child usually has difficulties with the learning of phonics. The learning of the many irregularities in the English language also often produce difficulties. The phonic approach would probably be accompanied by the learning of rhyming words and analogies such as 'would' and 'should'. There has even been an attempt to use a different simplified alphabet known as the *Initial Teaching Alphabet* (ITA), although ITA appears now to have faded from the scene.

Most teachers today would recognize the value of combining all methods. As reading is basically a system of obtaining meaning from letters we call symbols, an appropriately graded reading scheme would also be introduced. Books with pictures would be introduced in order to maintain interest as well as giving practice in following the rules learned earlier.

Published programmes for teaching dyslexic children

The controversial view that dyslexia may not be a weakness after all but merely a different way of learning is still being debated.

However, those writers who subscribe to this view have been stimulated into devising visual teaching programmes. Perhaps the most famous of these visual teaching programmes was devised by Davis and Braun (2003) and outlined in their famous book *The Gift of Dyslexia*. When confronted with a problem, dyslexic children are encouraged to think in images. This means seeing the 'whole picture' before being able to concentrate on the details. Among other writers who have devised similar visuo-spatial teaching programmes is Silverman (2004). He describes dyslexic children as 'visual-spatial learners'. Silverman asserts that children with dyslexia remember what they see but do not so easily remember what they hear. It is not that their hearing is impaired but rather that their listening skills are not as good as their visual memories. Also, it is interesting that Silverman and Freed (1997) have observed that dyslexic children are especially competent at reading non-verbal signals in people. This ability is also known as being able to read 'body language'.

There have been several kinds of multi-sensory programme developed over the years suitable for teaching dyslexic children. The Gillingham–Stillman method referred to in Chapter 1 was the forerunner of several of these teaching methods based on the multi-sensory approach. Perhaps the most popular of these programmes since that time has been the Hickey Multisensory Language Course (Combley, 2000). This is a programme that is often used by adults as well as by children. It was developed originally by Kathleen Hickey, a former Director of Studies at the Dyslexia Institute, and combines the learning of phonics with the learning of a sight vocabulary. Although the multi-sensory approach is recommended specifically for teaching dyslexic children, they are often used successfully with children who do not have literacy difficulties. The ordinary class teacher probably uses the multi-sensory approach just as widely as the teacher of dyslexic children.

Remediation based on possible cerebella deficits

There are two popular exercise programmes based upon the research evidence that deficits in the cerebellum are probably related to learning difficulties. The first of these is the Brain Gym founded by Dennison (1981). It consists of 26 physical activities and aims to develop children's physical coordination, their concentration, their memory and their literacy skills. Unfortunately, research into Brain

Gym results has not yet appeared in peer-reviewed journals so it is difficult to be able to recommend the programme for dyslexic children.

A second, more recently established programme, is the Dore programme, established by Wynford Dore (2006). Dore was motivated to devise the programme through having a child with dyslexia. Unlike the Brain Gym programme, the Dore programme was devised originally with the specific aim of helping dyslexic children. Since its inception, it has been developed and expanded and now claims to help children with ADHD, dyspraxia and Asperger's syndrome, as well as those with dyslexia. With such extravagant claims it is not surprising that many parents have shown an interest in it.

The Dore programme is based on the theory that literacy difficulties are the result of an imbalance between the cerebellum and the cerebrum. It claims to be able improve literacy skills through restoring the pathways between these two parts of the brain. As with the Brain Gym, it consists mainly of physical exercises to improve balance and coordination.

Unlike other exercise-based programmes, however, the Dore programme has been subjected to various research studies. The results from these studies suggest that parents should be cautious in enrolling their dyslexic children in the Dore programme at this stage of its development. There have been many criticisms. The results of a recent evaluation by Reynolds et al. (2003) appeared at first sight to be promising as significant gains were recorded on postural stability, phonological skills, vocabulary and semantic fluency. Reading gains, however, were notably small and could have been the result of factors other than those involved in the programme. Since then the Dore programme and its evaluation results have been heavily criticized by several authors. Ramos et al. (2003), Snowling and Hulme (2006) and Bishop (2007) have all criticized the research's experimental design. These authors say that the Reynolds et al.'s (2003) experimental design did not have an adequate research base or a satisfactory control group. Also, a study by Rochelle et al. (2006) concluded that 'defects of balance' are unlikely to be associated with dyslexia anyway. It seems that not all dyslexic children have problems with balance or with coordination. While future developments and further research might well produce a different picture, at this stage of its development, the claims for the Dore programme must remain 'not proven'.

Teaching the child to read at home

Whenever children are having difficulty in learning to read, there is a natural tendency for many parents to try to teach their children at home. This immediate reaction should be resisted. While there is little doubt that parental encouragement at home has a positive influence on the scholastic progress of their children, the first step should be to discuss the problem with the children's teacher.

As discussed in Chapter 4 there are many reasons, apart from dyslexia, why a child may struggle with learning to read. Whatever the possible causes of the problem, the teacher will know how best to start to investigate the child's difficulties. It would be only after the reasons for the problems are identified that the child's teacher might suggest ways in which parents can help at home. At this stage, the most useful thing parents can do is to avoid communicating any anxiety to the child.

While the details of what to teach are best left to the school, parents do have a part to play in reinforcing what is taught at school. In particular, the learning of pre-reading skills at school can be reinforced informally at home through participation in everyday family activities. Children with dyslexia usually have difficulty mastering pre-reading skills. Where children have not been able to acquire the necessary pre-reading skills, the teacher may well suggest that parents use various fun activities to help develop these skills. The child can learn to differentiate between left to right through being asked to help set the table for a meal. The parent demonstrates by setting one place and asks the child to copy with the other places, saying at the same time, 'We put the knife on the right side', and so on.

The skill of auditory discrimination can be reinforced at home with fun activities, such as the reading of nursery rhymes and the 'I-Spy' game. Practice in using the telephone is another favourite method of teaching the child auditory discrimination.

When competent in the pre-reading skills, there are countless opportunities in everyday life for increasing the child's sight vocabulary. Reading traffic signs and labels on food jars and cereal packets at breakfast time are a few examples of ready-made material for increasing the child's reading skills. It is important that all these activities are done in a positive, encouraging and fun atmosphere. They should not be introduced in such a way that the child is put under any pressure to achieve.

Developing language skills

The development of language involves not only the learning of a vocabulary but also the ability to communicate. These two processes have been called the learning of 'receptive' and 'expressive' language. Teachers and parents should take every opportunity to extend children's language and also their vocabulary. It could be said that words are the tools of intelligence. There is some evidence to show a relationship between the development of language skills and literacy. Children who are slow to develop language skills have been seen later to have literacy difficulties (Scarborough, 1990).

In order to become a fluent reader children need not only to have learned a minimum sight vocabulary, but also to have developed an adequate language facility. They have to be able to derive meaning from the spoken word before being able to derive meaning from the written word.

Children's language skills are developed through four modes– talking, listening, writing and reading. Dyslexic children are usually slow to develop these language skills, especially if taught in the traditional way. Children with dyslexia need to 'overlearn' all the rules of language; that is, they usually require several repetitions of new material and lots of practice, preferably within a 'fun' atmosphere.

Teachers and parents together play a significant role in developing language skills in children although the process has usually begun well before the child starts school. Children's language development begins at home with parents and siblings talking to them, routinely reading to them, listening to them and playing with them. Meetings with and playing with other children at school and outside the home continue this process.

Play is a natural, enjoyable activity for all children. Also, it can be a useful medium in which parents and teachers can develop children's language. For instance, they can introduce the prepositions by asking children to place objects 'up', 'down', 'behind', 'near', and so on all done of course in an informal, fun way.

The experience of being read to by parents plays an even more significant role in the development of the child's language. There is ample evidence to show the value of parents reading to their children and the value of homes where books are a common sight. There is little doubt that one of the best ways to prepare children for school is to show them picture books and to read aloud to them the stories that they like best. Children from the kind of background where parents regularly read to their children have a distinct advantage over children who come from homes where this does not occur. It is during the pre-reading stage that most children first make the important discovery that these squiggles we adults call letters and words are linked to the spoken word. Dyslexic children generally are no different in this respect, although some children with dyslexia may have a very short attention span. It is as well to be prepared for the dyslexic child losing interest early in the story-telling. If this happens, no further pressure should be put on the child to listen. The parent should merely accept the situation. In addition to the possibility of a short attention span, it may well be that the language contained in the story is too advanced for the child at that stage. This is not to say that new words should not be introduced. In fact, it is a good idea to gradually introduce the child to a few new words in a story as long as the story is interesting. Their vocabulary can be increased as children usually learn words that they have never heard before in this way. This assumes that the story maintains their interest. They can usually guess the meaning of a new word from the context. If they cannot guess the meaning of the word, most children will ask what the word means.

Reading to children is normally a pleasurable experience for parents as well as for their children. Both parents and their children come to look forward to a 'book at bedtime'. Children whose parents read to them in this way are not only helping their children increase their vocabulary but also teaching them that reading is pleasurable. The children learn to associate the reading of books with pleasure and so when the teacher introduces them to books in school, they are immediately reminded of the pleasure it has brought them at home.

It is important that children learn that reading is not merely a decoding activity. Once they learn that letters and words have meanings, the activity of reading stimulates the child's curiosity and then most of them want to learn to read themselves and so come to school highly motivated to do so.

Developing vocabulary through conversation

The child's vocabulary is increased, not only by story-telling, but also by talking to adults. It is important that the adult tries to extend the child's vocabulary through normal conversation. When a question is asked, the parent should try to pose open-ended questions that require further elucidation. This is preferable to just asking what are called 'closed questions' that require only one word answers such as 'yes' or a 'no'. As the child replies, the parent could introduce another word calculated to cause the child to question its meaning. A new word may be introduced to the conversation that is an alternative word to the one already used. An example would be the use of a new word like 'escape' when the conversation has been about running away from something. The child may have said, 'I feel like running away when you try to brush my hair.' The parent could reply, 'So you want to escape, do you?' Conversations like this may not only extend the child's vocabulary but also give practice in logical thinking.

Developing working memory

As just described, parents normally help their children to develop their vocabulary through everyday conversation. Parents can also help their children to develop their working memories through conversation. Most dyslexic children have a weakness in short-term memory. Parents may, for example, ask their children to recall a previous event, such as what they did the previous weekend.

It is not always appreciated that accurate remembering is partly dependent on the efficiency of the initial learning period. Whenever a child appears to be unable to remember something, it is a useful task to consider whether the initial learning was sufficiently strong. This process is termed 'strengthening the initial learning'. Attempts to help a dyslexic child remember grammatical rules, for instance, should focus on displaying the rules through all their senses as well as ensuring that the child is sufficiently motivated to remember the material. They should sound the rule, write the rule and perhaps draw it as a picture. It can be unproductive to ask a child to remember an event without having being sufficiently motivated to remember it in the first place. The child has to be interested in the material to be remembered. That way the initial learning will be strong and the child will be more likely to be sufficiently motivated to remember the material.

There have been several attempts to support children with weak working memories. Gathercole (2008), for instance, describes a recently devised teaching approach for supporting children with weak working memory. The programme encourages teachers to use memory aids such as charts and posters as well as computers and tape-recorders. A more structured approach is also described by Gathercole (2008). This is a computerized training program giving intensive practice with a series of memory tasks. Gathercole (2008) reports that evaluation of the program has revealed positive results among children diagnosed as ADHD as well as those with weak working memories.

Teacher expectancy effect

An aspect of teaching that is often neglected is the *expectancy effect*. This refers to the research evidence that most children tend to behave according to the teacher's belief in their worth. Teachers who might not understand dyslexia and who may even be unaccepting of the concept can have a negative effect upon a dyslexic child's performance. This is best exemplified by the research of Rosenthal and Jacobson (1968) who showed how teachers' expectancies affect children's progress. In a now famous experiment, they divided a group of mixed ability children into two classes, allocating a teacher to each group and giving each teacher different information. The teacher of group A was told that all the children in that group were of low ability so not much progress was expected. The teacher of group B was told that their group consisted of very bright children who were expected to make excellent progress. At the end of the term each group had attainments according to the information given to the teachers. Group A had made very little progress and group B had raised their levels of attainment. Rosenthal and Jacobson received much criticism over their experimental design but other research workers have since repeated this study using an improved design and have obtained similar results (Hargreaves, 1972).

Additionally, teacher behaviour can be unconsciously influenced by their expectations of children with learning difficulties in a mixed ability class (Good and Brophy, 1984). The following observations of teacher's behaviour were recorded:

- They tend to pay less at attention to them and smile at them less often.
- They tend to call on them less often to answer a question.
- They tend to demand less work from them.

These results do serve to alert all teachers to the dangers of operating with preconceived ideas of their pupils' lack of ability to make progress. Provided teachers fully understand the concept of dyslexia and are prepared to help the child with dyslexia, there is no reason why the expectancy effect need be a negative one.

Paired reading

Teachers usually feel that most children require a minimum amount of time spent on the learning of pre-reading skills before they will be ready to be introduced to formal reading material. Many children, however, arrive at school already proficient in them. Once a child has become proficient in pre-reading skills, further progress depends primarily on the development of their language skills. With adequate language skills together with the necessary pre-readings skills the reading process quickly becomes automatic.

It is in the initial learning of the pre-reading skills that the dyslexic child often experiences difficulties. Once the child possesses these pre-reading skills and adequate language, it may be that the teacher feels that the child simply requires more practice with a particular level of reading. In that case, the teacher might simply recommend that the parent listen to the child reading one of the school reading books at home. If this is suggested, it should be done in a relaxed atmosphere.

There is a particularly excellent method that parents can use to develop their children's interest in reading as well as their vocabulary. This method is known as *paired reading* and was devised and developed by Topping (2001). The details of this scheme are outlined below.

1. A book should be selected and approved by the child's teacher as being appropriate to the child's level of reading maturity. It should also be interesting to the child and sufficiently challenging. In other words, it should be neither too hard nor too easy.
2. The child and the parent begin by reading the book together out loud. As soon as the child is reading fluently and not stumbling over the pronunciation of any words, the child taps the table.

3. The tap is the signal for the parent to stop reading while the child continues to read aloud alone.
4. As soon as the child stops at a particular word, finding it difficult, the parent should wait no longer than five seconds before giving the child the word and then continuing to read aloud with the child. There must be no attempt to sound out the letters in the word that the child finds difficult or to comment on their difficulty.
5. At the end of each page the parent should praise the child's efforts.

An important feature of the paired reading approach is that children are reading for meaning and so are more likely to find reading pleasurable. Also, regular praise without criticism is highly motivating. The paired reading approach is particularly useful for dyslexic children as the system enables them to read at their own pace.

Summary

Reading is a complex process and consists of many sub-skills. It is in the learning of these reading sub-skills that dyslexic children often find difficulty. The development of language skills in the child is probably the most important of the pre-reading skills and so is usually the main focus of teaching in the child's early years. Teachers generally employ a variety of activities to help develop all these pre-reading skills in children. As dyslexic children usually have difficulties with these activities, this is when the child with dyslexia is often first identified. This chapter showed how dyslexic children might be helped to develop their literacy skills both in school and in the home. Many parents feel that they should help their children at home with pre-reading activities as well as with the skills of reading. While there is a role for parents in this respect, caution is advocated over attempting to teach the child at home without first consulting the child's teacher. Also, it is important that parents help their children at home in a relaxed atmosphere. Once children have reached the stage of being ready for formal reading, the tried and tested method known as 'paired reading' is recommended to help dyslexic children at home. Finally, over the years there have been several publicized innovative methods of teaching reading. Dramatic claims for their efficacy have been made for some of them, especially for those devised specifically for helping dyslexic children. Many parents are naturally attracted to these new methods. However, caution is advocated before the adoption of any new method of teaching dyslexic children. Whatever method is adopted, it is generally recognized that dyslexic children learn best with a multi-sensory approach to teaching. Most teachers in the ordinary schools generally use this approach for all children.

6   The causes of dyslexia

Introduction

During the early history of dyslexia, there was very little empirical research into the causes of dyslexia. There was a lot of theorizing and debate but without any scientific studies of the problem. Research into dyslexia today is very different, with the professions of medicine and educational psychology using empirical methods as well as sophisticated statistical techniques. Summaries of significant research into the causes of dyslexia, as well as into the remediation of dyslexia, are presented in this chapter.

Much of the empirical research into the causes of dyslexia has focused on the association between phonological processing and dyslexia and the differences in brain structures between dyslexics and non-dyslexics. The conclusions from this research using the functional magnetic resonance imaging (fMRI) and the positron emission tomography (PET) techniques to investigate brain functioning and dyslexia are outlined. Deficits in cognitive functions, such as weaknesses in working memory and confused laterality, are also discussed. Some evidence for visual processing deficits is also presented. Finally, in this chapter, the evidence that dyslexia may be a difference in functioning rather than a deficit is explored. The chapter begins by outlining some of the evidence for dyslexia being of genetic origin.

Genetic factors

Dyslexia had long been seen to run in families. There was always the suspicion that it was inherited, although there was no scientific evidence for this until recently. There is now evidence to demonstrate that dyslexia is indeed likely to be an inherited. Fagerheim (1999) established the existence of a relevant gene on chromosome 2. Grigorenko (1977) found that chromosomes 6 and 15 were linked to a weakness in phonological awareness, which is a common characteristic of dyslexia. Finally, Fisher and Smith (2001) have identified genes on chromosome 15 as commonly found in children with dyslexia. Although the possession of these genes makes dyslexia more likely, it does not necessarily follow that children with a dyslexic gene will automatically develop dyslexia. As has been concluded with gene research into other areas, the identification of a particular gene does not guarantee that the gene under survey will necessarily be actively responsible for a particular piece of behaviour. Environmental factors also play a part. Behaviour is not a function of either heredity or environment alone. Behaviour is always a product of both heredity and environment. However, gene research into the origins of dyslexia is persuasive and does suggest that the child with the identified gene is more likely to be dyslexic.

Functional magnetic resonance imaging and positron emission tomography

Alongside the search for the genes responsible for dyslexia a different, but no less dramatic, research was taking place in a different direction. This research was focusing on the identification of different brain functions between dyslexics and non-dyslexics. The localization of different brain functions became possible as a result of the development of fMRI and PET. The use of this technology has revolutionized research into brain functioning. Through the fMRI and PET techniques it has become possible to measure the blood flow in particular parts of the brain and, by photographing this activity, determine how much that part of the brain was being activated. Using this equipment, empirical evidence for a neurological basis for dyslexia appears to have been established. One example of this is the discovery of an association between dyslexia and weaknesses in *phonological analysis*. Using the fMRI technique it has also been shown that the area of the brain concerned with phonological analyis is not as well activated in those with dyslexia, as it is in the case of normal readers (Shaywitz, 1996).

It has long been observed that many dyslexics have weak working memories (McLoughlin et al. 2002). With the use of the fMRI technique it is been possible to verify this observation. The site of working memory in the brain has been mapped and differences between dyslexics and non-dyslexics in the activation of this area have been seen. There are different kinds of memory and they are all found to be located in the frontal lobes of the brain in both the right and the left hemispheres (Carter, 1998).

Although these medical techniques appear to have shown differences between dyslexics and non-dyslexics in memory functions and also in the functioning of other parts of the brain, caution should be used in applying these results uncritically. One reason for caution is that the different functions located in the brain rarely work in isolation. As the brain works *in toto,* whatever sensory input is activated, it has to be processed by the whole cortex. An example of this is when referring to the *visual area* of the brain. In fact, there are many visual areas in the brain with each one specializing in a different aspect of vision. The information transmitted from each of these areas is processed separately.

Phonological processing

Phonological processing is the term given to the ability to associate sounds with letters and also to be able to break down words into their sounds. It has now been established that the skill of phonological processing is a basic skill in the reading process. The significance of phonological processing in learning to read is now firmly established, and also the observation that children with dyslexia find particular difficulties in the learning of this skill (Snowling, 1995; Snowling, 2000).

Research, particularly by Snowling (2001) and Nicolson and Fawcett (1999), has illustrated the kind of difficulties dyslexic children experience in the learning of phonological processing. It seems that dyslexic children have difficulty not only with retaining phonological information but also with attaching verbal labels to the material. Fluent readers automatically retrieve necessary phonological information from their long-term memory store. Dyslexic children have difficulty doing this owing to their weak working memories. Nicolson and Fawcett describe children who cannot do this as 'lacking automaticity'. They view dyslexia as being primarily the result of deficits in certain parts of the cerebellum that cause problems with the automatic acquisition of phonological skills.

It has become clear from the results of the above-mentioned research that many dyslexic children rely more on learning the meaning of words through their total shape rather than by sounding out the letters and trying to blend them into a whole. This is probably because they have difficulty remembering the letter–sound associations. As pointed out by Snowling (1995), children with dyslexia will always have a problem with words they come across for the first time. This difficulty manifested by many dyslexic children has also been noticed by Gathercole and Baddeley (1990). As children have to retrieve phonological information from their long-term memory store, dyslexics inevitably will have problems with new words. Non-dyslexic children rely on their long-term memories to access phonological information in order to spell new words and dyslexic children cannot easily do this. Goswami (1991) has also noted this difficulty, emphasizing that a good working memory is required in order to access appropriate word blendings. Papagno et al. (1991) observe that this is probably the reason why dyslexic children usually learn to read primarily by associating words with their meanings. It appears that the dyslexics' difficulty with phonological analysis is likely also to be the main reason for their spelling problems.

Differences in hemispherical functioning

There is evidence that the different hemispheres of the brain are activated with different tasks (Springer and Deutsch, 1998). Although, in practice, the brain works as a whole entity, it has been shown that the left side of the brain is more involved than the right side of the brain in the development of general language skills and also with phonological processing (Galaburda, 1989; Shaywitz, 1996). When children learn to read, there is evidence that they tend to use mainly the left side of the brain, *the temporal plana*. In contrast, the right side of the brain seems to be more involved in visuo-motor activity and visual creativity. The differences in function of the two hemispheres is particularly relevant to children with dyslexia as it seems that there is an unusual balance in dyslexic people between the two hemispheres (Galaburda, 1989). In Galaburda's study of adults with dyslexia the temporal lobes showed either symmetry or else the right side was larger than the left side. This is in contrast to non-dyslexic adults whose temporal lobes generally showed asymmetry, that is, with the left hemisphere larger than the right. Although the Galaburda research was conducted with adults, there is no reason to assume that children would be any different in this respect. Best and Demb (1999) also found that while most non-dyslexic people's left and right brain hemispheres were asymmetrical, dyslexic brains showed symmetry, thus giving further support to Galaburda's conclusions.

From these research findings it would seem that dyslexic people probably use the right side of their brain more than their left side and are likely to be more comfortable doing so. As the right side of the brain is more concerned with analysing and processing visual information and with creative processing (Geschwind and Galaburda, 1985), it seems likely that dyslexic children are going to be happier developing their creativity and their facility for analysing visual phenomenon than in developing language skills.

However, if children with dyslexia do have difficulty with left brain activity, it would not be unreasonable to assume that they are more at ease with right brain activity. Consequently, it should mean that children with dyslexia would be happier to be involved with subjects such as art and art-related subjects, which depend on the visual, spatial and creative areas of the brain. Anecdotal evidence would seem to support this view, as there appear to be a disproportionately larger number of students in art colleges who are dyslexic. However, some other studies to date on this topic have shown conflicting results (Schultz et al. 1994). The topic continues to be debated.

Although the evidence for the link between hemispheric asymmetry and dyslexia is persuasive, it is not yet clear whether the asymmetry of the two hemispheres is responsible for dyslexia or a consequence of it. Schultz et al. (1994) advocate caution against drawing the conclusion that dyslexia is caused by the asymmetry of the brain until it has been firmly established.

Laterality

As previously discussed in Chapter 2, a common sign of dyslexia in children is a difficulty in learning their left from their right. This is usually accompanied by a tendency to reverse letters such as 'b' and 'd'. Herbert et al. (2005) consider that the tendency to reversals is a function of the asymmetry of the brain. All children have a difficulty with this until around the age of 6 or 7. However, most children eventually establish dominance of eye, hand and leg and have a tendency to prefer either their left side or their right side. Which side they prefer is dependent on which hemisphere in the brain has developed the dominance (Harris, 1979). Some children may never establish dominance and this does not prove to be a problem to them as they are equally at home with both sides. These are the children called 'ambidextrous'.

In dyslexic children, however, the problem of establishing dominance tends to persist and to remain a problem, sometimes continuing into adulthood. These people never properly establish dominance and so there is always a slight delay if asked to respond to left or right. We call this process 'confused laterality'.

An interesting area of research is the relationship between left-handed dyslexic children and speech. There is evidence that a higher proportion of dyslexic children are left-handed (Geschwind and Behan, 1982). Furthermore, there is some evidence that speech, in about one-third of left-handed children, is located either in the right hemisphere or in both hemispheres. This is in contrast to right-handed people where spoken language is located usually in the right hemisphere.

Magnocellular deficits

Magnocells are large neurones situated on the cerebellum part of the brain. They are responsible for the synchronization of auditory, visual and motor activities. It has been discovered that dyslexic children are often deficient in these magnocells (Stein and Walsh, 1997).

A deficit in magnocells might mean that there would be problems with the synchronization of events such as visual tracking while reading. Eye movements would be out of synchronization with the perceived visual input. This is a common characteristic of a dyslexic child (Borsting, 1996). It would also cause slowness to read as well as a tendency to confuse the order of words and letters. The regulation of temporal events, such as setting a pace when walking, or throwing a ball in a particular direction, are also often seen in dyslexic children. Problems in these areas may also be the result of deficits in magnocellular structures. Difficulties with the delivery of speech and deficits in working memory have also been seen to be associated with deficits in magnocellular structures. The manifestation of these deficits can be seen in dyslexic children who sometimes find that their thinking is quicker than their speech. They know what they want to say but often it takes an abnormally long time to find the right words to express what they want to say.

There have been attempts to remediate this kind of temporal difficulty in dyslexic children through using computer games. As a deficiency in magnocells is said to cause slowness in the speed of processing information Tallal et al. (1997) conducted an experiment in which they allowed a dyslexic child more time to respond to stimuli and with practice the child was seen eventually to improve in phonological processing skills.

Cerebellum activity

It has long been known that the cerebellum in the brain is responsible for coordinating physical activities such as movement and balance. As described earlier in this section, Nicolson and Fawcett (1995) have demonstrated a link between dyslexia and deficits in the cerebellum language area of the brain. Further to this research, Nicolson and Fawcett (1995) have shown also that there is an association between phonological problems and motor skills. These authors have demonstrated that dyslexic children often have difficulty with balancing as well as in the estimation of time. Their work is of practical importance for teachers as they have devised tests to assess possible dyslexia in children through measuring a child's phonological and motor skills as well as their literacy attainments (see Chapter 7).

Deficits in the cerebellum region of the brain have also been seen to cause difficulties with the pronunciation of certain words (Kirby and Drews, 2003).

Despite the research indicating an association between dyslexia and cerebella inactivity, it is by no means certain that impairments in the cerebellum are the direct cause of dyslexia. However, in view of the persuasive research evidence to date, it would not be surprising to discover eventually that there is a direct link between impairments of the cerebellum and dyslexia. Although this direct link has still to be satisfactorily established, it would not be unreasonable to conclude that the cerebellum has a major role to play in the manifestation of dyslexia through problems with general organization and motor skills, as well as through difficulties with the learning of literacy skills. This has led to some interesting work over the years into attempts to develop a child's language through physical movement. This work is discussed in the next section.

Weakness in working memory

There are different kinds of 'memory'. At the risk of oversimplification of this concept, there are four kinds of memory: auditory memory (memory for sounds and how to process them), visual memory (memory for letter and word shapes), kinaesthetic memory (memory for the 'feel' of things like shapes and textures as well as memory for time), and semantic memory (memory for the meaning of words). Working memory consists of the interaction of all four of these modes. This can be illustrated by reflecting on the different kinds of memory involved when processing a mental arithmetic problem that is presented orally.

There is ample research evidence to assert that a weakness in working memory is a common characteristic of children with dyslexia (Rack, 1994) and Stanovich et al. (1997), and Gathercole and Baddeley (1990). As described earlier, dyslexic children usually have difficulties also with phonological processing. It has been suggested that a weak working memory underlies the problems children demonstrate with phonological analysis (Pickering, 2000; McLoughlin et al. 2002). In other words, is the observed weakness in working memory a direct cause of dyslexia or is it simply a reflection of their phonological difficulties?

As pointed out by McLoughlin et al. (1994), as dyslexic children have difficulties with phonological analysis, they are inevitably slower to read aloud than when reading silently. Reading silently does not require them to remember the sounds of the words. It seems that children with dyslexia concentrate more on trying to remember the meanings of words than they do on trying to remember the sounds made by the words (Papagno et al., 1991). They also cannot easily attach verbal labels to pictures. This means that when young dyslexic children are first introduced to picture books they inevitably are slow to understand what they are trying to read.

It is difficult to find evidence that a weakness in visual memory might also be related to dyslexia. However, an unpublished study by the author of a sample of 726 adult students with dyslexia discovered that most of them were below average on a test of visual sequential memory.

Dietary factors

An interesting recent area of research has been that into the influence on mental functioning of dietary supplements. One example of this kind of research has been into the effects of the addition of Omega-3, a fatty acid supplement, to a child's daily diet. It is claimed that some children are deficient in this acid and including it in the diet can improve reading attainment (Portwood, 2002). Further research may eventually substantiate these claims but to date the evidence is not totally persuasive.

Dyslexia as a difference and not a deficit

The notion that dyslexia is a *weakness* had always been assumed until a very different view of dyslexia began to emerge in the early 1980s. Some authors began to view dyslexia not so much as a weakness, but rather a *different* way of learning. This view was first propounded by Gardner (1983) with his theory of multiple intelligences. He pointed out that there are other kinds of intelligence as well as the linguistic kind. As a result of this theory the traditional view of intelligence as a single process of logical and linguistic thinking increasingly came under scrutiny. Gardner suggested that there are eight different kinds of intelligence. He asserted that children might show intelligence in other directions such as drama, dance and the arts in general, and yet that these other pursuits are rarely valued to the same extent as a logical linguistic ability. He suggested that the traditional focus in schools on fostering logical thought through the linguistic medium might be doing a disservice to some children who possibly had talents in these other directions. Gardner asserted that dyslexic children in particular were being penalized in this way. The eight intelligences proposed by Gardner are as follows:

- linguistic intelligence;
- mathematical intelligence;

- spatial intelligence;
- kinaesthetic intelligence;
- musical intelligence;
- interpersonal intelligence;
- naturalist intelligence;
- logical/mathematical.

It is interesting to note that Gardner's original theory that people have different kinds of intelligence has now been developed and incorporated into classroom activities in some schools in the USA (Armstrong, 1994; Lazear, 1994).

A research topic that appears to give support to the view that dyslexia might be a difference is the research into *learning styles*. A learning style is said to be a consistent and habitual way of learning and processing information. The most popular researched learning styles cited are the sensory styles: auditory, visual and kinaesthetic. The child with a visual learning style is said to learn best through pictures, diagrams and perhaps with full use of an overhead projector. The child with an auditory learning style would learn best through listening and talking. The child with a kinaesthetic learning style would learn best through being active, using a hands-on approach.

The range of identified learning styles proposed in the literature is considerable. Among these were the cognitive learning styles concerned with problem solving (Bruner et al. 1960). In problem solving, it seems that some children take a reflective view of the information and think about solutions whereas others might prefer to adopt a more 'hands-on' practical approach to the problem. Again, some children learn best through taking a global approach when tackling a new problem while others seem to prefer to work in stages tackling one part at a time. Some children prefer to focus on one part of a problem while others prefer to scan the whole. Bruner et al. (1960) described children with these different learning styles as 'focusers' and 'scanners'.

It is hypothesized that people learn best when encouraged to use their preferred learning style. In a study by Dunn et al. (2000), teaching students in colleges through their identified learning styles appeared to improve their academic achievements. Unfortunately, at the present time research evidence for the existence of different learning styles appears to be contradictory. Stahl (2002) asserts that there is no evidence that children do learn in different ways. Mortimore (2003), on the other hand, gives evidence to the contrary. Although the notion of matching children's learning to their identified preferred learning style is an attractive one, Mortimore (2005) also advocates caution in the adoption of this approach. Despite the various claims for its value, it seems that its efficacy with dyslexic children has yet to be satisfactorily established. Learning style theory needs to provide more empirical evidence before it can be universally accepted. Common experience demonstrates that children use all their senses when learning, although perhaps with different emphases given to each at different times, depending on the task. For example, some might use sight more than sound so learn more efficiently through visual information. There are others whose preferred mode of learning might be auditory so they would learn more efficiently listening to a teacher and then discussing it.

Despite the conflicting research evidence, some colleges have introduced computer screening designed to identify dyslexic students by assessing their unique learning styles. It is hypothesized that those with a more visual learning style are more likely to be dyslexic.

The notion that dyslexia is not a deficit but merely a difference is an attractive one and perhaps future research will provide further evidence for dyslexia as a difference rather than a deficit. To date, however, the verdict on dyslexia as a difference has not yet been satisfactorily resolved.

Summary

It has long been observed that dyslexia 'runs in families' but the research has now firmly established that dyslexia is of biological and genetic origin. However, it would also appear from the results of this research that the causes of dyslexia are unlikely to be found in any single area. There appear to be a multitude of possible causative factors involved. For instance, it has been suggested in the research that dyslexia may originate in the child's genetic make-up, their phonological processing deficits, their working memory weaknesses, hemispherical imbalances, magnocellular deficits, neurological impairments and visual processing difficulties, as well as in environmental factors such as a lack of appropriate learning experiences. Moreover, all these different functions have the capacity to interact with one another. It would seem, therefore, in the light of this research evidence, that it may well be a fruitless task to try to isolate any single cause of dyslexia.

A relatively recent debate has centred on whether dyslexia may not be a deficit after all but merely a different way of learning. Some evidence for this view comes from the work on multiple intelligences and learning styles. It is suggested that people termed dyslexic are penalized through society's strong emphasis on literacy skills. This is no doubt true, as communication in society takes place mainly through the written word. Some evidence suggests also that dyslexic people are particularly creative. While these are optimistic and encouraging views, they may ultimately prove to be valid but at this stage more empirical research is needed before they can be universally accepted.

7 Assessing dyslexia

Introduction

Parents often wonder what kind of tests will be used when their children are referred for an assessment for dyslexia. This chapter sets out to allay any anxieties that parents may have if their children are referred for an assessment for dyslexia and describes some of the most popular tests used in the assessment. The rationale for their selection is also discussed. As a result of the recent expansion of training courses for teachers on the topic of dyslexia, an increasing number of teachers are now qualified to formally assess dyslexia and to use tests that previously were on restricted usage. The chapter outlines the tests that can be used by teachers without needing to possess special testing qualifications, as well as those tests on restricted usage.

There are occasions when teachers may consider it necessary for children to have more detailed assessments than they are able to provide themselves. After discussing this need for further assessments with the children's parents, teachers might refer the children to either educational psychologists or teachers with special qualifications in dyslexia. The chapter begins by outlining the screening procedures teachers may use if they suspect dyslexia in a child. The checklist as a popular screening test for indications of possible dyslexia is the first test discussed.

Checklists

Teachers are most usually the first to notice signs of dyslexia in a child. Whenever a child is seen to be having literacy difficulties and there is no obvious reason for it, it would not be unreasonable to consider the possibility of dyslexia. Although eventually a formal assessment by a qualified professional may be required, an initial screening device like a checklist is often a useful starting point. There are several such checklists in existence. One of the popular ones is presented in Appendix II.

A checklist usually consists of a number of the most common behaviours seen in the child with dyslexia. In the usual checklist a tick is placed next to each one of the behaviours that is considered to apply to the child in question. The greater the number of items ticked, the more likely it is that the child has dyslexia.

Although there is a role for checklists, their results should always be interpreted with care. First, as dyslexia is always a matter of degree, there is no sharp cut-off point when deciding whether the results indicate dyslexia. This makes it difficult to decide from a checklist result if the problems are sufficiently severe to take the step of requesting a more detailed assessment by a professional trained in the assessment of dyslexia.

A further difficulty in interpreting the results of a checklist is that dyslexia shares many of the same behavioural signs as shown by children with other specific learning difficulties, as discussed in Chapter 4. Many other specific learning difficulties that show similarities to dyslexia can wrongly indicate dyslexia on a checklist. For instance, a child who had been showing symptoms of attention deficit hyperactivity disorder (ADHD) would give positive replies to many of the questions on the checklist such as, 'Do you find prolonged concentration difficult?' or 'Do you easily forget oral instructions?' Only an individual testing with appropriate materials and administered by a suitably qualified professional could accurately differentiate between the person with ADHD and the person who is dyslexic.

So a checklist can give both false positive and false negative results. The results can show that children are dyslexic when, in fact, they may not be dyslexic and also the converse; they may show that children are not dyslexic when, in fact, they are dyslexic.

Despite these criticisms, checklists do have their place in diagnosing dyslexia. A checklist is particularly useful as a method of preliminary screening when it is necessary to identify those children in a large group who may be at risk of dyslexia.

Individual tests

An individually administered test is likely to be a more reliable assessment procedure than a checklist. Among the more popular individual tests available to teachers is the *Bangor Dyslexia Test* (Miles, 1982). The Bangor Dyslexia Test was designed for use with children from 7 years of age up to the age of 18 and is specifically designed to identify signs of dyslexia. Among the abilities tested are laterality and auditory/visual sequential memory. This is an excellent individual test and can be obtained for use by non-specialists.

A recently updated screening test also available to teachers is the *Dyslexia Early Screening Test (DEST 2)* devised by Fawcett and Nicolson (2004). It offers a more intensive testing programme than the Bangor Test. Dyslexia is identified through an assessment of both motor and linguistic skills. The test is standardized on children aged 4 years and 6 months to 6 years and 5 months.

A recently standardised test designed to identify particular areas of literacy difficulties is the *Dyslexia Portfolio* (Turner, 2008). This test is described by the publishers as for pupils who have already been screened and seen to have signs of dyslexia. This assessment procedure comprises eight short tests and assesses reading, spelling, phonology and digit span. The test is available to specialist teachers and is standardized for use with children aged 6 to 16 and takes approximately 40 minutes to administer.

Self-administered tests

Computer-based assessments are becoming increasingly popular. An example of this is the *Dyslexia Screener* (Turner and Smith, 2006). Computer assessments are particularly useful for children who may be nervous of an individual testing situation and who are happy with the computer. The Turner and Smith test comprises six tests of three types. The three areas sampled are comprehension (verbal and non-verbal), reading and spelling attainment and phonological processing with speed of information processing. It is standardized for use by children aged from 5 to 16 years.

As with screening tests, caution is advocated in interpreting the results of any self-administered test. This is mainly because these tests require the child to be relaxed and properly motivated. These conditions are not necessarily ensured if children test themselves. Many children with dyslexia find prolonged concentration difficult and so are more likely to give up on a self-administered test before the test is completed. In an individual test session they can be encouraged to relax and to continue to persevere if they begin to show fatigue. The skill of the tester is a key factor in ensuring adequate motivation and a relaxed testing environment. Research has consistently shown that it is possible to obtain more reliable test results with individual testing than is possible with any of the screening procedures discussed so far in this chapter.

Assessing intelligence

When assessing a child for dyslexia it is useful to know the child's level of intelligence. The first reason for assessing intelligence would be to rule out the possibility of a general learning difficulty. It is also important to assess whether there is a discrepancy between reasoning ability and other abilities, such as working memory. Intelligence is most reliably assessed through tests of general ability like the *Wechsler Intelligence Scales for Children* (WISC). Screening procedures may provide a rough estimate of intelligence but are never quite as reliable as individual assessments of general abilities. Unfortunately, the WISC test is on restricted usage. The WISC is described in more detail in the following section.

Another useful battery of tests that is often used in the assessment of dyslexia is the *British Ability Scales* (Elliot, 1997), although again on restricted usage. This battery of tests gives measures of general ability and reasoning ability as well as attainments in literacy and numeracy. A feature of the British Ability Scales battery is that it enables the assessor to select appropriate tests for the difficulty under investigation, without needing to administer the whole battery.

For teachers who are not able to take advantage of the specialist courses allowing them access to the above tests, there are several other tests available to them that are often equally useful. Among these is the *Raven's Progressive Matrices* devised and standardized by John Raven (1998). It has been used worldwide for the last 30 years and its popularity continues. This test is particularly useful for dyslexic children as it is relatively unaffected by language difficulties. It consists of a series of pages each containing a visual pattern with a piece missing. The task is to find the missing piece from a series of other patterns. It is said to provide a measure of general intellectual ability but is probably best considered as a test of non-verbal reasoning ability. It is also useful in that it is not affected by lack of educational experiences as much as the other intelligence tests. Accordingly, it measures what has become known as 'fluid intelligence'. The test usually takes about 30 minutes to complete.

An assessment of these non-cognitive factors is often relevant when deciding if a child should be considered dyslexic, or should perhaps come under some other category of learning difficulty. An assessment of self-esteem, locus of control, anxiety levels and general motivational states are often important variables to be tested contributing to the final assessment of dyslexia. An assessment of the influence of non-cognitive factors is usually made in the light of the psychologist's clinical experience. However, clinical judgement may sometimes need to be supplemented by appropriate standardized tests.

Defining intelligence

Before describing intelligence testing it is important to be clear on what is meant by the term 'intelligence'. There has been voluminous research into the nature of intelligence over the ye   ~~ ᵈ ꜛ⁺ ꜛ~ ᵖrobably true to say that this topic has been the object ol   ,   )n and controversy than any other single topic in edu   ᴐology. Intelligence testing in particular has been a vas. ____   arch for decades, for both psychologists and educationalists. Many different definitions of intelligence have been offered and many different tests to measure intelligence have been devised.

In order to define intelligence it may be helpful first to say what is 'not' intelligence. It is not an entity in the brain like a muscle that can be made bigger through training. Intelligence is not something that can be viewed under a microscope. In fact, it is probably more accurate to regard intelligence not as a 'thing' but more as a way of behaving. So, it is probably better to refer to 'intelligent behaviour' rather than 'intelligence'. However, for simplicity's sake we can still use the word intelligence. Although it is not possible to separate completely the effects of heredity from environment, there is strong evidence, through identical twin studies, that the greater part of what we mean by intelligence is inherited. However, although heredity may set the limits of the development of intelligent behaviour, there is no way of knowing *a priori* what those limits will be. In teaching, therefore, it is usually assumed that the limits of development of intelligence have not been reached. It used to be thought that the level of intelligence in an individual was fixed at birth. It is now known that intelligence test scores can increase on a retest after a period of intense intellectual stimulation. The converse can also happen; a person will show a decrease in scores after a prolonged period without intellectual stimulation. Clearly, environmental influences play a significant part in the development of intelligence.

Measuring intelligence

In everyday life we all seem to know intuitively what we mean by intelligence. When we say a person is intelligent we are usually referring to their quality of reasoning, speed of thinking, capacity for understanding things quickly and their problem-solving ability. These abilities can be measured in both the verbal sphere and the non-verbal sphere. Intelligence tests have been devised to measure both verbal and non-verbal problem solving. The tests are then administered to large samples of people of different age groups and average scores are then calculated for each age level. This makes it possible, when subsequently measuring an individual's intelligence, to compare their scores with the average scores of others of the same age.

A valid intelligence test is dependent on how far the tests really do measure what we mean by intelligence. This is known as the validity of the test and the degree of validity can be measured. Intelligence tests measure different things depending on the type of activities that are included in the tests. This is why defining intelligence has historically been difficult and has led to the view in some quarters that intelligence is simply 'what intelligence tests measure'. This may sound like a somewhat facetious definition of intelligence, but it also contains a grain of truth as different intelligence tests often measure different aspects of what we call intelligence.

Wechsler Intelligence Scale for Children (WISC-IV)

As defined in Chapter 1, dyslexia is manifested in many different ways and the person with dyslexia can display weaknesses in several different intellectual functions. It is important, therefore, when assessing for dyslexia, to obtain measures of all these different aspects of intellectual functioning. This is especially important for dyslexic children as in this way their strengths as well as any specific weaknesses can be identified. These abilities are often measured by the WISC-IV, which is probably the most used of all the tests of intelligence, and has been regularly revised since it was first introduced in 1949. The latest revision was in 2003.

There are 14 subtests in the WISC, each measuring a different intellectual ability. The 14 subtests can be divided into 7 verbal tests and 7 performance (non-verbal) tests. Three separate IQs can be calculated from the results of these subtests. Thus it is possible to calculate a verbal IQ, a performance (non-verbal) IQ and a full-scale IQ. The results from all the subtests are aggregated to obtain the full, or global IQ. The individual test items and explanations of the abilities that they measure are listed below.

Verbal tests

Vocabulary test

This test requires definitions for a series of words presented orally and in order of increasing complexity. It reflects individual cultural experiences that include reading experience. It is also dependent on working memory.

Similarities test

This test measures the ability to explain what two words have in common. It is measuring verbal concept formation and verbal reasoning ability.

Arithmetic test

This test requires the solving of a series of arithmetic problems presented orally and with increased difficulty. The items are timed. The test is measuring working memory as the subject has to retain the information and then be able to process it.

Digit symbol test

This test consists of two lists of orally presented number sequences. Each number series is increasing in length. The child is asked to recall the first series forwards and the second series backwards. It is measuring both auditory rote memory as well as auditory sequential memory.

Information test

This test consists of a series of general knowledge questions presented orally about factual information. It reflects a child's cultural background and it is also a measure of long-term memory.

Comprehension test

This test consists of a series of orally presented questions designed to measure the child's ability to obtain practical solutions in social situations. It has been referred to as a test of common sense. As most of the questions are lengthy in their administration, it is also dependent on working memory.

Letter–number sequence test

This test consists of an orally presented series of numbers and a series of letters. The child is asked to repeat the numbers and letters giving the numbers first in numerical order and the letters second in alphabetical order. Like the digit span test, it is a measure of working memory.

Non-verbal tests

Picture completion test

This test consists of a series of coloured picture cards, each with an important part missing. The child has to identify the missing piece. It is a measure of visual perception and attention to detail as well as being dependent on long-term memory.

Digit symbol test

This is a pencil and paper test. It consists of a series of numbers each of which has a blank square beneath it. The child is given a key containing a symbol for each number. The child is then asked to fill in the blank squares with the corresponding symbol from a key. The test is timed and is a measure of the speed of processing visual information, fine motor coordination and visual sequential memory.

Block design test

This test consists of nine coloured blocks. The child is asked to construct geometric patterns with the blocks copied from designs presented on a separate card. The items of the test have to be completed within a specified time. It is a test of visuo-spatial organization and visual problem solving. The literature considers this test to be a measure of non-verbal reasoning ability and the speed of processing visual information.

Matrix reasoning test

This test consists of a series of cards each containing coloured patterns. Each of the patterns has one piece missing. The child is asked which one of a series of five other smaller patterns is the missing piece. This test is also considered to be a measure of non-verbal reasoning ability. Its successful performance is often adversely affected if the child has any kind of visual defect or lateral confusion.

Picture arrangement test

This test consists of a series of three to seven cards, each containing a cartoon picture. The child is asked to arrange the cards in their logical sequence to tell a story in a fixed period of time. It is a test of visual sequential thinking.

Symbol search test

This test consists of a series of five symbols at the end of which there are two other symbols. The child is asked to mark 'Yes' or 'No', using a pencil, if either of the two symbols is seen to be present in the line of symbols. The test is timed and so is a measure of the speed of processing visual information. It also reflects fine motor coordination ability.

Object assembly test

This test requires the child to complete a series of jigsaw puzzles of common objects. It is a measure of visuo-spatial organization and the ability to form visual concepts.

Calculating indexes

The latest revision of the WISC-IV is of particular interest when assessing for dyslexia. This new revision allows for the analysis of the results into four factors known as *Indexes*. The test results are combined as follows:

Factor one

A *verbal comprehension* index is obtained by combining results from the following subtests:

- Information
- Similarities
- Vocabulary
- Comprehension

Factor two

A *perceptual organization* index is obtained by combining results from the following subtests:

- Picture completion
- Picture arrangement
  - Block design (or symbol search)
    - Object assembly

Factor three

A *working memory* index is obtained by combining results from the following subtests:

- Arithmetic
- Digit span

Factor four

A *processing speed* index is obtained by combining the results from the following subtests:

* Coding
* Symbol search

An IQ can still be calculated from these results if required, but this new way of calculating indexes is more useful when assessing children who are dyslexic. A dyslexic child's specific learning difficulty can be more easily identified and recorded separately from the child's verbal and non-verbal intelligence.

Other tests of cognitive functioning

Working memory

Although it is possible to make an estimate of working memory ability from the WISC test results, a more detailed assessment of working memory can be obtained from the *Working Memory Test Battery for Children* (Pickering and Gathercole, 2001) or the *Automated Working Memory Assessment* (Alloway, 2007). Moreover, both these tests are available to teachers without having to take a special course in testing. These tests have distinct advantages over the WISC. Both tests assess working memory as well as non-verbal memory and are not so dependent on verbal skills as are the Wechsler tests.

Phonological assessment

Research has consistently shown a relationship between phonological processing ability and literacy skills. An analysis of the child's phonological skills therefore is an important part of the assessment when investigating possible dyslexia. There are several tests available for use by teachers for the assessment of phonological skills. One example of these tests is the *Phonological Assessment Battery* devised by Frederickson et al. (1997). This battery of tests consists of five subtests and has been standardized on children aged between 6 and 15 years. These are an alliteration test, a rhyming test, a naming speed test, a fluency test and a spoonerisms test. The research suggests that most dyslexic children have some difficulties with the abilities measured by these tests. For instance, it is not uncommon to come across children with dyslexia who tend to use spoonerisms in everyday life, much to their embarrassment. The spoonerisms test is a particularly useful test in this battery. The child is asked to deliberately devise a spoonerism as, for example, when asked to exchange initial sounds in two words as in 'car park' would become 'par cark'. This task can prove difficult for children with a weakness in phonological analysis ability. A second test to assess phonological skills is the *Phonological Abilities Test* devised by Muter et al. (1997). This test contains four subtests and is standardized on children aged between 5 and 7 years.

Laterality tests

Dyslexic children often reverse letters and also sometimes reverse the order of words in sentences. Those who show this characteristic are said to have a degree of lateral confusion. This behaviour is normal with children up to around the age of 5 or 6 who will tend to use both left and right hands interchangeably. However, by the age of 8 most children have usually established dominance for one hand over the other. They will also have developed one eye more dominant than the other so that if looking through a telescope, for example, they would put it to the dominant eye. Eventually most children will learn to distinguish left from right. However, there is evidence that there is often a slight delay when having to do so in children with dyslexia. For instance, if asking children with lateral confusion to turn to the left, they might hesitate before they actually turn left. This confused laterality is also commonly manifested in dyslexic children being slow to process written work as well as in the occasional reversal of the order of letters when spelling.

There are standard tests of laterality available such as the *Harris Tests of Laterality* (Harris, 1979), but the assessment of possible lateral confusion is usually carried out informally during the assessment. There are several ways in which laterality can be assessed informally. Children would be asked to perform a series of tasks that demand the choice of left or right. One of these tasks, for example, would be to look through a hole in the middle of a piece of paper and then slowly to bring the paper onto their face while continuing to look through the hole. The task for the assessor is to observe which eye the children use when the paper is brought right onto their face. The eye chosen will be their dominant eye. Those who are dyslexic are likely to be unsure which eye to select and may show confusion. A further test for laterality might be to ask the children to point with their left hand to their right ear and instruct them to do the opposite. Again, children with lateral confusion will demonstrate a marked delay in choosing. Some children have a dominant eye that is opposite from their dominant hand. So, for instance, they may have their left eye dominant but are right-handed and vice versa. These people are described as being crossed laterals. It used to be thought that crossed laterals would always be dyslexic. It is now known that this is not so. In several studies investigating the topic, the results have shown that there as many crossed laterals among people with dyslexia as there are among those who are not dyslexic. It is *confused laterality* that is commonly associated with dyslexia and which causes a delay when having to select left from right.

Literacy tests

Tests of reading attainment, spelling attainment, speed of reading and speed of writing are usually administered when assessing for possible dyslexia. Children with dyslexia are usually slow to read, particularly if asked to read out aloud. Spelling attainment is also often a problem. This is because spelling ability places demands on phonological abilities. It is important to know the children's precise levels of attainments in reading and spelling in order to determine if they require remedial help in these areas.

Reading attainment is usually measured in three different ways: word recognition, comprehension and speed. A silent comprehension test and an oral comprehension test are usually administered where dyslexia is suspected. There is often a difference in their performance between these two different tests of reading comprehension. Usually children with dyslexia are able to process reading quicker when reading silently than when having to read aloud. The *Spadafore Diagnostic Reading Tests* are suitable for testing both silent and oral reading comprehension. Another well-standardized test of reading comprehension is the *Watts-Vernon Reading Test*. This test consists of 35 sentences with the final word in each sentence omitted. The task is to select the missing word from five alternate choices.

Examples of suitable tests for assessing word recognition and spelling are the *Wide Range Achievement Tests* (WRAT) and the

Woodcock Reading Mastery Test (WRMT). The third edition of the WRAT, WRAT3, is the result of 60 years of development and has two particularly useful features. First, it gives a measure of reading, spelling and arithmetic skills. Second, each of these three measures comes in two alternate forms. This means that each battery of tests can be administered before and after any teaching without having to repeat the same tests. The tests have been standardized on ages from 5 to 75 and so can be administered to children and adults. Finally, an important feature of the WRAT3 is that the test results are quoted in standard scores with the same standard deviations as the WAIS III. This means that its results are often helpful if used in conjunction with the WISC test results when planning a remediation programme.

Speeds of reading and writing are usually slow in dyslexic children. Both these skills are dependent on working memory. Reading speed can be assessed through the presentation of various lists of words. The *Neale Analysis of Reading* is a well-standardized test, popular not only for testing reading comprehension and word accuracy but also for measuring reading speed.

The assessment

Cognitive abilities are usually tested first and they generally form the main part of an assessment for dyslexia. It is difficult to be precise regarding the time taken for a full assessment for dyslexia but normally it should take no more than three hours. The time taken will vary largely according to the speed of working, the intelligence of the child being tested and the degree of cognitive weaknesses shown.

Teachers and psychologists who assess children for possible dyslexia are usually well aware of the need to establish rapport with the child before introducing the tests. It is essential that the child being tested is sufficiently relaxed in order to ensure a reliable test result. Occasionally, however, an anxious child may find it difficult to relax in one session so that it may be necessary to arrange a second assessment session. By the time the child has relaxed there is not sufficient time to complete the assessment. Another circumstance that may necessitate the arrangement of a second session would be if the child refuses to cooperate. In that case the test session may need to be abandoned altogether. The child's emotional state as well as a lack of motivation might well be significant factors in their learning difficulties. In that case, it would be planned to assess these non-cognitive factors, as well as the usual tests of cognition, in the second session. The main tests used to assess non-cognitive factors are discussed in the following section.

Assessing non-cognitive factors

Non-cognitive is the term given to the emotional and motivational aspects of personality to distinguish them from the cognitive, or intellectual, aspects like intelligence and memory. Anxiety levels, self-esteem and locus of control are among these non-cognitive factors that may need assessment. Non-cognitive factors are important variables that determine how far a child will be properly motivated to perform well in the test. All these factors can affect test performance.

As described above, there are many reasons why a child might not be properly motivated to obtain a reliable test result. Anxiety was mentioned as one factor that might interfere with a child's motivational state. It is generally accepted that a modicum of anxiety is necessary for the successful completion of any task. However, it is well known that too much anxiety interferes with clear thinking and also with memory.

There are other factors that can be measured that also can affect test results. It is one of the skills of testing to be able to identify these other factors and then to make allowances for them. For instance, a temporary mood, test familiarity or undue fatigue will affect performance on most intellectual tests.

Some non-cognitive factors such as self-esteem and locus of control can be measured with standardized formal tests. However, when assessing for dyslexia most non-cognitive factors are more likely to be assessed through observation of the child's general responses to the test session. The non-cognitive factors that can be measured are discussed below.

Self-esteem

A person's level of self-esteem is a major non-cognitive factor that can affect test results. There is ample research evidence indicating a correlation between people's level of academic attainment and their self-esteem level. Consequently, it is always desirable to assess self-esteem. The topic of self-esteem is discussed in more detail in Chapter 9.

The main object of the dyslexia assessment is to obtain cognitive measures and the person being tested is subjected to intensive intellectual effort in the process. It may be unfair therefore to subject them also to additional formal self-esteem testing. This is why, in general, self-esteem would be more likely to be assessed intuitively and based on observed test behaviour. However, if there were grounds for believing that low self-esteem is markedly affecting test performance, then a second session might have to be arranged during which self-esteem would be formally assessed.

Locus of control

Locus of control is another non-cognitive factor that can affect test results and which research shows to have a correlation with academic achievement. External locus of control was defined in Chapter 2 as one of the characteristics of the child with dyslexia.

Once again, it would be unfair to routinely subject children being tested for dyslexia to a formal testing of their locus of control, in addition to the cognitive testing. Accordingly, the psychologist would make a clinical judgement of the child's locus of control during the test session. However, if there was a suspected problem with locus of control, then as with the need to measure self-esteem a second test session would have to be arranged.

Summary

Parents often ask what tests are used to assess for dyslexia. Teachers are usually the first to suspect dyslexia in a child and a checklist of symptoms is a popular tool that teachers can use to assess children for signs of dyslexia. Although an easy method to use, caution is expressed in interpreting the results of screening tests for dyslexia as these procedures have only a limited degree of reliability. Self-administered computer tests are popular among children, especially where a child is inclined to be over-anxious during an individual assessment. However, it is generally recognized that a one-to-one individual assessment administered either by a specialist teacher with training in the assessment of dyslexia or an educational psychologist is the most reliable method of assessment.

It is considered important to obtain a measure of a child's present level of intellectual functioning, or intelligence, when assessing dyslexia. Just as with the definition of dyslexia, the definition of intelligence continues to be debated. Different intelligence tests measure different aspects of what is known as intelligent behaviour. The WISC is probably the best standardized as well as being the most reliable of its type for this kind of measure. The latest revision of the WISC is particularly useful for assessing dyslexic children as it gives separate measures on reasoning ability, working memory and the speed of processing information. Dyslexic children tend to have significant discrepancies between reasoning ability and the other two factors.

Other cognitive tests, such as tests for assessing literacy and laterality, are also required when assessing a child for dyslexia. It is important to know the kind of errors children make when reading, writing and spelling.

Tests of a non-cognitive nature are often used to supplement the results of the WISC. Non-cognitive factors can contribute to motivation and so influence test results. These non-cognitive tests involve measures of self-esteem, locus of control and anxiety and are most often assessed informally during the formal testing of cognitive abilities. In conclusion, although the ordinary class teacher and sometimes a parent are sometimes able to identify signs of dyslexia in a child, it is only through using the tests described that dyslexia can be reliably confirmed.

8 Understanding a psychological report

Introduction

Understanding a psychologist's report can be a challenge to those who are not familiar with psychological terminology and are not acquainted with the particular statistics used in the report. The psychologist's report is generally sent to the school that referred the child for the assessment. On occasion some parents may ask to see the report. Additionally, there are parents who may have asked for a psychological assessment privately and will receive the psychologist's report. This chapter helps teachers and parents who are not specifically trained in special education to know how to interpret a psychologist's report. The tests and the statistics used in the interpretation of the test results are presented. A detailed description of the tests most frequently used by psychologists is provided.

While most parents would be happy for their child to be assessed by a teacher, a referral to an educational psychologist may be intimidating. The very title *educational psychologist* can be a source of anxiety for some parents. One of the aims of this chapter is to allay any anxieties parents may have in this direction by explaining the role and qualifications of the psychologist.

Following the assessment, parents and teachers often ask to know a child's intelligence quotient (IQ). This chapter explains why the quoting of an IQ after an assessment of a dyslexic child can be misleading and so is rarely used. After assessing a dyslexic child, four indexes are usually quoted instead of the IQ to better represent the test results. These indexes are outlined and also the rationale for preferring them to the traditional IQ. The chapter begins by discussing the role of psychologists and their qualifications.

Qualifications of an educational psychologist

While most parents easily understand the role of the specialist teacher, they may not be so familiar with the work of an educational psychologist. It is not uncommon for parents to be anxious about their child seeing a psychologist for the assessment. Just as with the concept of dyslexia itself, many people are unsure exactly what to expect from a psychologist. It often helps to allay their anxieties knowing the role and qualifications of an educational psychologist.

The training of an educational psychologist takes a minimum of seven years. The first part of their training is a university course leading to a degree in psychology. The next step for new graduates in psychology who wish to qualify as educational psychologists would be to obtain a teaching qualification.

The teacher training is usually followed by a minimum of two years of successful teaching. Until recently their final qualification was a post-graduate degree in educational psychology. In addition, some universities are now offering three-year full-time training to doctorate level. This training is usually followed with a post in a local authority psychological service where the psychologist works under supervision. Once the period of supervision is completed the psychologist is eligible to apply for Chartered Status and can apply for a Practising Certificate issued by the British Psychological Society. The educational psychologist is now qualified to practise. This Practising Certificate has to be renewed annually with evidence that the psychologist has engaged in approved professional development activities during the past year.

A qualified psychologist would be an educational psychologist whose name appears on the *Chartered List of Psychologists*. This list is maintained and published by the *British Psychological Society* (*BPS*). The aim of this document is to protect the public from employing a psychologist who may attempt to work in this applied area of psychology without possessing the necessary qualifications. Copies of the document are available in public libraries throughout the UK. The psychologists named in this document would have the letters *C. Psychol* placed after their names. There are stringent regulations governing the use of these letters and only those with approved BPS training are eligible to use them. A list of all qualified psychologists, including educational psychologists, can be found on the Internet, classified according to the geographical regions in which they work.

The work of an educational psychologist is greatly varied and the topic of assessing for dyslexia may be only one area of specialism. It would be rare for an educational psychologist to agree to administer an assessment of dyslexia without adequate training and appropriate experience in this area.

A dyslexia assessment conducted by an educational psychologist is often preferred because of their additional training and experience in the assessment of emotional and motivational factors. As stated in the previous chapter, these factors can easily influence the results of the cognitive testing. There are also other learning difficulties that can be confused with dyslexia and it would be rare for a specialist teacher to be trained in the assessment of these other conditions.

Why the IQ is misleading for dyslexic children

The WISC usually forms the essence of a psychologist's report. As described previously, the WISC was developed as a measure of a child's intelligence through the calculation of an intelligence quotient. However, an IQ is likely to give a false impression of intelligence in a dyslexic child. The reason for this false impression is that in order to obtain the IQ, all the subtest scores in the WISC are added together and among these scores there will inevitably be lower subtest scores reflecting the child's dyslexia. For instance, the dyslexic child often has relatively lower scores on subtests measuring working memory and the speed of processing information. In contrast to these results, subtests measuring reasoning ability are usually higher than the scores obtained on subtests measuring working memory and the speed of information processing. If an IQ is calculated from the WISC and included in the report, it can easily be misinterpreted and cause distress for the parent as well as for the dyslexic child.

Despite the risks of misinterpretation, the recording of the IQ is warranted in particular circumstances. For example, it would be useful for providing necessary evidence in cases where the assessment results did not indicate a specific learning difficulty. This would apply if all test scores were below average with no indication of a specific weakness in any particular area of ability. In this case, the child's learning difficulty would be described as a general learning difficulty as opposed to a specific learning difficulty.

Indexes as an alternative to the IQ

Intelligence comprises several different abilities. The latest revision of the WISC sets out to group these different abilities into four spheres of intellectual functioning. These four distinct categories are termed *indexes*. Two of these indexes give an estimate of the child's reasoning ability while the other two report working memory and the speed of processing information. With the calculation of separate indexes the child's intelligence (defined as reasoning ability) can now be assessed separately from their weaknesses. As the mean score on each index is 100, calculating each of the indexes is tantamount to recording four different IQs. The four indexes are explained below.

WISC indexes defined

The four indexes usually recorded in the psychologist's report are verbal comprehension, non-verbal comprehension, working memory and the speed of processing information. The indexes are compiled and recorded after an analysis of the scores obtained on the subtests. Children's strengths as well as specific areas of weakness can be identified more easily with the four indexes. It can be reassuring for parents and children to know that even if children have weaknesses in specific areas of ability, they also have strengths. For example, even if they have literacy difficulties, their logical reasoning ability, often considered to be 'intelligence', may be within normal limits. It is reassuring to know that the reason for children's literacy problems is not lack of intelligence. The following description of the four indexes lists the subtests in the WISC as described in Chapter 7.

1   Verbal Comprehension Index (VCI)

The VCI is considered to be a valid measure of verbal intelligence. The scores that are to be added together to calculate this index are from the following subtests:

- Vocabulary
- Similarities
- Information

2 Perceptual Organization Index (POI)

The POI is considered to be a valid measure of non-verbal intelligence. The scores that are to be added together to calculate this index are from the following subtests:

- Picture Completion
- Block Design
- Matrix Reasoning

3 Working Memory Index (WMI)

This index is a measure of working memory and particularly auditory sequential memory. The scores that are to be added together to calculate this index are from the following subtests:

- Arithmetic
- Digit Span
- Letter–Number Sequencing

4 Processing Speed Index (PSI)

This test is a measure of both visual sequential memory and the speed of processing visual material. The scores that are to be added together to calculate this index are from the following subtests:

- Digit Symbol Coding
- Symbol Search

Index scores are calculated by adding together the scaled scores of specific subtests as described above. They have an average range from 90 to 110 as with the traditional intelligence quotient.

Understanding the statistics

Interpreting the statistics in a psychological report can be daunting at first sight as it often contains the use of terms and statistical phrases that are not in everyday use. Some psychologists, in addition to recording the test results, also include statistics relating to the construction of the tests. It is suggested here that the practice of recording statistics other than those relating to the individual's test scores is not necessary in order to understand how dyslexia has been confirmed. Ideally, the reporting of statistics should be kept to a minimum for the ease of interpretation of test results.

Many people are bewildered by statistics. The subject can be a difficult one, especially for people with little knowledge of mathematics. However, some statistics have to be quoted if the test results are to be made meaningful. It is important, for instance, to know how far the scores obtained are above or below the rest of the population. This information helps teachers and parents to know how severe the children's weaknesses are as well as their strengths.

Parents and probably many teachers will be relieved to know that it is not necessary to have studied statistics in depth in order to understand the basic terms and figures quoted in the psychologist's report. It is also not necessary to know how to calculate statistics in order to understand what they mean. Moreover, there are only four basic statistical terms that need to be understood when interpreting the psychologist's report on dyslexia. These are 'means', 'standard scores', 'percentiles' and 'index scores'. These four terms are defined below. For those who may wish to know how to calculate these statistics, a fuller interpretation of these statistical terms can be found in most statistical handbooks.

The mean score

The mean score refers to an average score. Mean scores are calculated by adding together thousands of children's test scores (also called 'raw scores') and then dividing them by the number of children tested. This has been done in the WISC with children at each age level from aged 5 to 16. These means are recorded in the WISC test handbook.

By looking up a child's score in the appropriate table in the handbook, we can determine where that score stands in comparison with other children of the same age. We would find a mean score given for other children of the same age of the individual concerned. All the index scores are based on a mean of 100. The average range on the WISC is between 90 and 110; therefore, any score below 90 would be considered to be below average. Any score above 110 would be considered to be above average.

Standard or scaled scores

For ease of interpretation, standard scores are also averages obtained from transposing the individual's raw scores. The raw scores made by the child are not normally recorded in the psychologist's report. These scores are adjusted for age and are then reported as standard or scaled scores. This process is called 'transposing' the raw score. The standard scores or scaled scores on the WISC each range from 0 to 19. The average standard score for each subtest is 10.

Percentile rank

The WISC tests have been administered to thousands of children of various ages. In the interest of ease of further understanding test results, percentile rank scores are sometimes also calculated. These percentile rank scores are based on the results of a hypothetical sample of 100 children.

The percentile rank refers to the number of children who would be expected to score at and above a given percentile. So a percentile score of 95 would mean that if the same test were to be given to 100 children, there would be 95 who would obtain a lower score. By the same token, there would be only 5 who obtain a higher score. As with the mean statistic, the percentiles scores are found in the test handbook. A percentile statistic and a standard score are usually recorded in the psychological report.

Table 8.1 illustrates the relationship between standard scores and percentile scores in a normal population.

Table 8.2 illustrates the classification of index scores and percentages of the population in each category.

Table 8.1 Illustration of the spread of standard scores and percentile scores in a normal population

Standard scores	55	70	85	100	115	130	145
Percentiles	1	2	16	50	84	98	99

Table 8.2 Illustration of the classification of index scores and percentages of the population in each category

Classification	Index score	% of the population
Very superior	130 and above	2.2
Superior	120 to 129	6.7
High average	110 to 119	16.1
Average	90 to 109	50.0
Low average	80 to 89	16.1
Borderline	70 to 79	6.7
Extremely low	69 and below	2.2

An example of a dyslexic child's WISC test results might be recorded with indexes and percentiles to look like the example in the Table 8.3.

In Table 8.3 there is a marked discrepancy between the two indexes that measure verbal and non-verbal intelligence (the VCI and POI) and the two that measure Working Memory and Speed of Processing (the WMI and SPI). It would be safe to conclude from this example that the child tested had a very superior ability in verbal intelligence (VCI) and a superior ability in non-verbal intelligence (POI). In contrast to these high scores, their scores on the remaining two indexes are well below average. This would be considered to be a typical dyslexic profile.

The pattern of results quoted above would confirm dyslexia. These results would suggest that children would easily understand new material, as their intelligence is high but the chances are,

Table 8.3 Example of WISC index scores and percentiles illustrating a typical dyslexic profile

WISC Indexes	Index scores	Percentiles
Verbal Comprehension (VCI)	140	99
Perceptual Organization (POI)	125	95
Working Memory (WMI)	86	18
Speed of Processing (SPI)	78	7

without appropriate help, they would have difficulty remembering it and also they would be slow to process it.

Literacy scores

Literacy scores are usually given in terms of reading and spelling ages. However, reading and spelling test results are sometimes presented in standard scores or scaled scores. The raw scores are transposed into standard scores at each age level. The average range is 90 to 110.

Interpreting test behaviour

The importance of the psychologist establishing rapport with the child to be tested was discussed in the previous chapter. In the process of establishing rapport with the child, the assessor would need to be aware of non-cognitive factors that could affect the test results. In most cases it would be unlikely that there would be non-cognitive factors affecting the results, so there would be little of significance to report. However, children sometimes become anxious when under test conditions and this behaviour can affect their test performance. If undue anxiety appeared to have affected the results, the psychological report would contain a separate heading to record this fact. In addition to anxiety affecting test results, self-esteem and locus of control are well-known non-cognitive factors that can affect motivation to succeed in the test situation and these would also be recorded. Where the child's self-esteem and locus of control are formally assessed, it would be usual to do this with standardized questionnaires. These questionnaires' results are usually recorded with either standard scores or with raw scores presented in relation to a mean score.

Summary

When a dyslexia specialist has assessed a child, it is usual for the assessor to issue a formal report. However, unless the parent concerned works in the field of special education, much of the report can often be difficult to understand. The interpretation of a psychological report can be difficult even for a teacher. The reasons for this are, first, that without knowledge of statistics most teachers and parents would not find it easy to understand the test results. Second, the special terms used are not always familiar to the non-specialist. However, it is the statistics that parents and some teachers find the most difficult to understand. They need not be daunted as there are only four statistical terms that need to be understood. These four statistical terms are the mean, standard score, percentile and index score and their meanings are explained in the chapter. The recording of literacy test results is usually done in terms of reading and spelling ages, although sometimes test results are presented as standard scores or scaled scores. It is recommended that the child's level of intelligence should be recorded using the WISC Indexes. Traditionally, an intelligence quotient was recorded, but the Indexes are seen to more accurately reflect a dyslexic child's intellectual functioning.

An educational psychologist often administers the testing and it is understandable that most parents are curious about the qualifications and the role of this professional. This topic was discussed not only in order to satisfy parental curiosity, but also to allay any anxieties parents may have over their child being seen by a psychologist. It is essential that the educational psychologist has the required qualifications and experience and abides by the standards required to practise. The psychologist should be a Chartered Psychologist with a Certificate to Practice issued by the British Psychological Society.

9 Self-esteem and the dyslexic child

Introduction

Most people would agree that high self-esteem is a desirable personal characteristic. This is especially so with dyslexic children. Unfortunately, children with dyslexia are particularly at risk of developing low self-esteem. This is not only because they often feel inadequate when comparing themselves to other children, but also because as a result of the many frustrations that often accompany dyslexia. For instance, it is not easy to remain confident in front of other people if you are always forgetting what they say or are always slow to react. This can happen to dyslexic children both at home and in school. These frustrations may not only result in low self-esteem but also in dyslexic children developing behavioural problems.

There is evidence of a strong relationship between reading attainment and self-esteem (Lawrence, 2006). Children with high self-esteem usually do better in schoolwork than those with low self-esteem. Moreover, the relationship between self-esteem and scholastic attainment is reciprocal; low self-esteem affects attainment and low attainment affects self-esteem. Additionally, there is research evidence to show that high self-esteem is associated not only with scholastic attainments but also with emotional adjustment and sound physical health. So children who have high self-esteem are more likely to be healthier and happier, as well as having fewer behavioural problems.

These are the reasons why it is important that children with dyslexia are identified early and given appropriate help. With an understanding of the challenges they face and given appropriate support, the possibility of low self-esteem and behavioural problems arising will be diminished. This chapter describes these possible problems and suggests tried and tested strategies that teachers and parents can use to lessen the chances of them occurring. The chapter begins by defining self-esteem.

Definition of self-esteem

As with many concepts in psychology that are used in everyday life, self-esteem in psychology is defined in a specific way. Additionally, there are many misconceptions regarding what is meant by self-esteem so it is important to define this term precisely before discussing it any further. Self-esteem is best defined as *the evaluation of the discrepancy between a child's self-image and their ideal self.* The three concepts of *self-esteem, self-image* and *ideal self* together make up what we refer to as the self-concept. In order to understand how the three concepts are related, they are now defined separately.

Self-image

This is the image we have of our mental and physical characteristics. A person's self-image is formed gradually throughout life by 'bouncing off the environment' as we experience life in its many forms. Children first develop an image of themselves physically. It starts in babyhood as they gradually become aware of the different parts of their bodies. Gradually, through the behaviour of parents and other people who regularly communicate with them, children begin to develop an awareness of the kind of person they have become. Their self-image is being formed. The process of forming a self-image continues throughout childhood and into adulthood as people gradually become more conscious of themselves. By the time adulthood is reached, most of us have a good idea of our abilities and the kind of person we have become. The more experiences we have had, the richer will be our self-image. As with most things in life, there will be both positive and negative aspects of our self-image. We will have compared and contrasted ourselves both positively and negatively with countless other people during many contacts throughout life. We learn in so doing that there are some things in which we are competent and also some things in which we are not competent. We also learn the kind of person we have become; whether we are popular with others or not popular, for instance.

Children learn either that they are readers at one extreme or at the other extreme that they are non-readers. Those children who are dyslexic soon learn that they are not as proficient as many children when it comes to literacy skills. The more severe the dyslexia, the more negative characteristics they will attribute to themselves and they are more likely to have developed a negative self-image. This is why it is essential that parents and teachers are aware of this image that dyslexic children have of themselves. It is important that dyslexic children maintain a positive self-image so that they remain motivated to learn. Many children who are told that they are dyslexic will not fully understand what this means. Although perhaps most children take this news in their stride without undue concern, some will imagine that the word dyslexia means all kinds of unpleasant things. This is one reason why parents and teachers need to have a sound knowledge of dyslexia. Dyslexia should be explained to the child along with the positive aspects of dyslexia regarding their expected progress. If a negative self-image is allowed to develop, the dyslexic child will find it difficult to believe that they are able to learn.

Ideal self

The ideal self consists of our ideals and our sense of the ideal way of behaving. It contains the standards of behaviour and the particular achievements that are valued in the society to which we belong. It also comprises our levels of aspiration; the kinds of achievement we desire and the kind of person we would like to be. All these values are formed as we go through life. The formation of the ideal self begins in childhood as teachers and parents normally help children acquire the standards and morals of society in general. Most children begin to learn, for instance, that the adults around them value being polite and honest and caring for others. As well as these moral standards, children also learn that adults value certain skills such as being able to read and doing well at school. At first, children learn these values from others but as they grow older they gradually begin to form their own values. Some children may begin to identify with particular models in the media. These models can soon become part of their ideal selves, whether they are desirable or otherwise. The ideal self has then become a composite of learned moral values and ideal ways of behaving to which children aspire. Among these learned values is the ability to read and to do well in schoolwork. Young children quickly learn that parents and teachers value literacy skills so to be able to read gradually becomes part of their ideal self.

Self-esteem

Children's self-image and their ideal self normally will have developed side by side. This means that children eventually will have a perceived image of themselves and also an image of the kind of person they would like to become. Accordingly, there is a discrepancy, under normal circumstances, between the self-image and the ideal self. It is how we feel about this discrepancy that forms our self-esteem. Self-esteem can be defined as *the evaluation of the discrepancy between self-image and ideal self.* Most people generally accept that there is always room for improvement. It seems to be human nature for people to want to better themselves in various ways. People have an idea of the kind of person they are and also the kind of person they would like to be. Most of us have aspirations to improve ourselves in various spheres of life.

¶Children with dyslexia will normally be aware of the need to be able to read and to spell like the other children. Whether the discrepancy that exists between their current level of achievement and their aspiration to achieve affects their self-esteem will depend mainly on how the adults they respect react to their dyslexia. Wise parents and teachers will remain positive and react with encouragement. This means that the children's self-esteem will not be threatened. An unwise teacher or parent who overreacts, showing undue concern and communicating anxiety, is likely to reduce the child's self-esteem. Most children with dyslexia will usually care already that they are unable to read and to spell. They have learned that these skills are highly valued by teachers and by parents as well as by other children. Not being able to achieve their ideal self in this way places their self-esteem at risk. Without appropriate help, there will be prolonged failure and low self-esteem will soon develop.

The effects of low self-esteem are, first, a lack of confidence in their ability to learn and, second, feelings of inadequacy in general. Feelings of inadequacy with regard to literacy skills will eventually generalize to the whole personality. In other words, they eventually begin to feel failures as people and so begin to lack confidence in everything. The result of this is a lack of desire to learn anything new and even an avoidance of new experiences, believing that they will inevitably fail. This is when we also say they have 'low motivation' to succeed.

The self-concept as a motivator

The self-concept is formed through experiences as we go through life. A significant phenomenon of the self-concept is that not only is it determined through experiences but that to a large degree it also determines experiences. In other words, it is a motivator. We all tend to do the kind of things that fit in with how we see ourselves. Let us imagine that we are on holiday and are looking for a social club. We find ourselves walking past a tennis club on one side of the road and a sailing club on the other side of the road. Those of us who play tennis would probably choose the tennis club while the sailors among us would choose to visit the sailing club. In the case of children who see themselves as poor readers, they would avoid books and not see books as relevant. In addition, children with dyslexia whose self-concept comprises images of not being able to perform as well as other children are likely to feel some degree of insecurity when engaged in tasks that demand literacy skills. They are not motivated to seek out reading material. Good readers when entering a library are more likely to pick up a book and poor readers would be more likely to look out of the window or even avoid the library altogether.

Children with low self-esteem often feel anxious or insecure. In the case of dyslexic children, their self-image tells them that they are not able to perform academic skills as well as other children. Consequently, they may try to avoid situations that demand skills such as reading, writing or contributing to oral discussions. Dyslexic children who continue with a negative self-image often make excuses not to participate in work that causes them to feel inadequate. There have been instances known to the author where dyslexic children have said, 'I cannot do this work because I am dyslexic.' It is important that children with dyslexia are helped to develop a positive image of themselves, despite their dyslexia, otherwise they will develop not only low self-esteem but also what Seligman (1991) has termed 'learned helplessness'.

Expressing low self-esteem

The individual personality of the child determines precisely how low self-esteem is manifested. There is evidence for some basic personality differences being constitutionally determined (Eysenck, 1980).

There appear to be two particular personality dimensions that are believed to be of constitutional origin (Eysenck, 1980). Differences in these will determine how low self-esteem will be manifested. The first one is the *introvert/extrovert* dimension of personality. The more introverted child will prefer quieter pursuits and will be happiest when working or playing alone or perhaps with only one or two other people. The extrovert child, in contrast, will prefer more lively pursuits and will prefer the company of other children when working or playing.

This personality characteristic of introversion/extroversion can be measured along a continuum of behaviour. The introverts lie at one end of the continuum and the extroverts at the other end. The majority of children lie somewhere in the middle of the continuum and are neither extreme introverts nor extreme extroverts.

The second personality characteristic that seems to be of constitutional origin is *emotionality.* This is the extent to which people react with emotion. Again, this personality characteristic lies along a continuum with most people in the middle. However, some people tend to overreact emotionally when frustrated while there are others who tend to underreact.

When experiencing frustration, children will tend to react in terms of their individual personality characteristics as described above. Low self-esteem children who are extroverted will react in an outward fashion and if also emotionally reactive, this behaviour will be exaggerated. These children are likely to try to deny feelings of inferiority by being boastful and even arrogant. It is as if they are trying too hard to compensate for their feelings of inferiority. The more introverted, on the other hand, will react inwardly by being withdrawn in situations where they are at risk of showing their inadequacies. If inclined also to be emotionally overreactive, then the frustrated child is likely to develop anxiety and nervous behaviour.

Self-concept is resistant to change

It might be thought that merely challenging the negative self-image of dyslexic children would change it. This is not so, as one of the characteristics of the self-concept is that it is resistant to change. It is interesting to witness children with low self-esteem being praised for doing good work. For example, if they were given praise for a picture they had drawn, their reaction might be to tear it up, as praise would make them feel insecure. Perceiving themselves as worthy of praise conflicts with their self-image. Teachers and parents should be ready for this reaction and not be put off by it. It is essential that they continue to relate positively to dyslexic children even though some children may resist their efforts to encourage them. Provided parents and teachers are consistent and genuine in their praise, children will, in time, begin to accept it and their self-image will change.

Developing a positive self-image in the child

Not being able to keep up with the other children in class can be very frustrating for dyslexic children. It can cause them to feel inferior as they compare themselves with other children. If this continues, they soon begin to perceive themselves in a negative light. Being identified as dyslexic sometimes has a negative effect on children's self-image and can compound their feelings of inferiority. Children who are suddenly given the label of *dyslexia* inevitably wonder what it means. They often imagine it means all sorts of unpleasant things. They will certainly be aware that the label implies they are in some way different from other children. One example of a dyslexic child's imagination running riot is the case of the child who said to the author, 'Dyslexia means I have something wrong with my brain.'

It is essential that dyslexia should be explained to children. It is important that children are helped to see that dyslexia need not be a negative characteristic. The first step should be to explain to children that dyslexia is not an illness. The next step should be to explain to them that dyslexia means that their brain often works in a particularly creative way. If young children finds this explanation difficult to understand, the parents might explain to their children that nobody can excel at every task or skill and that all people have strengths and also some weaknesses. This may also be the stage when children's attention might be drawn to the names of dyslexic people who have become famous in other spheres than the linguistic one, for example, in sport, the arts and entertainment.

Emphasis on children's strengths is another method of helping the development of a positive self-image. In this regard, it is important that children's test results obtained during the assessment for dyslexia are discussed with them. The tests would have identified strengths as well as any weaknesses in the assessment. For instance, the dyslexic child will usually have scored higher on tests of reasoning ability and comprehension than on tests of literacy. There is a greater chance of the child's self-esteem being maintained as long as the child's highest assessment test results are highlighted.

As the teaching of linguistic abilities has traditionally had a major focus in the classroom, other abilities that children may possess are often underplayed. Many children succeed on the sports field or in the art room although not excelling in the academic sphere. Dyslexic children's self-esteem will continue to be at risk as long as society places such a high premium on linguistic abilities. Dyslexic children need to be continually reminded of the personal values of being kind to others, getting on with other people and being helpful to other people in life generally. With society's emphasis on achievement, personal values are often neglected. It is a salutary experience to reflect on the fact that humans have perfected their scientific techniques and ability to fly to the moon and yet are still unable to live peaceably with one another. It is not unnatural for parents to feel disappointed when their children fail to make progress. It is important that parents reassure their children that they are loved and valued as people even if they are failing in literacy skills.

Anxiety and low self-esteem

It has long been known that a small degree of anxiety is necessary for any learning to take place. It has also been known that too much anxiety disrupts performance. In addition to experiencing frustrations as a consequence of low self-esteem, some dyslexic children also experience undue feelings of anxiety over their failures. This is especially so if the child is by innate temperament inclined to be over-emotional. All children who regularly experience failure are at risk of experiencing some degree of anxiety. If severe, anxiety and stress experienced by dyslexic children can exacerbate their problem with working memory (Zatz and Chassin, 1985). As referred to above, feelings of anxiety disrupt performance. People in an argument who become emotional lose the argument as their feelings prevent them from thinking clearly. Children with dyslexia are more prone to experience anxiety and to experience it more severely as they inevitably have to encounter familiar failure situations. This is because of the process known as *conditioning.* It is an established psychological phenomenon that whenever two things have regularly appeared together, the future appearance of one of them tends to remind the person of the other one. So each time dyslexic children are placed in situations where they have previously failed, they are likely to remember the previous failures and to react with anxiety.

The concept of failure

There has been some discussion over the years in educational circles over the desirability of organizing teaching so that a child does not have to experience failure. It was proposed that this action would protect the child from developing low self-esteem. This notion is a further example of a misunderstanding over what is meant by self-esteem. To protect a child from a failure experience would not only be unrealistic but also deprive the child of valuable 'trial-and-error' learning. Children learn many skills through making mistakes and learning not to repeat them. More importantly, it is not failure itself that is the problem. It is the *attitude* that teachers and parents have towards the child's failure that can either lower or maintain the child's self-esteem. If children are regularly criticized for failing to achieve the standards demanded by the adults, then low self-esteem will follow. Their failure in literacy skills soon generalizes to their whole personality so that they begin to feel failure as people. If, on the other hand, they are encouraged and praised for their efforts, self-esteem will be maintained.

It is interesting that where children have high self-esteem, the evidence is that they are not so easily influenced by negative criticism. They are more likely to accept criticism objectively and do something about it and try to improve. It also seems that whether a child is affected by criticism depends on the credibility and status, in the eyes of the child, of the person doing the criticism. It follows that parents and teachers are usually in a powerful position in this respect. The child's peers also have an effect but their influence on the child's self-esteem comes later with the onset of adolescence.

Nobody can go through life avoiding failure. There will always be somebody, somewhere, who is more skilled, cleverer, more intelligent, and so on. In this sense, failure in all walks of life is inevitable. This is particularly so with children as in childhood much learning takes place through trial and error with inevitable mistakes in the process. As previously emphasized, it is not failure experiences *per se* that constitute a problem. It is the *attitude* towards the failure that is the key. In the case of the dyslexic child, it is the attitudes of the teacher and the parent that determine whether the child develops low self-esteem. This is especially so with the very young child who has not yet become self-determinate. With normal development, most children will also begin to compare themselves with others and so self-evaluation also occurs. The attitudes of parents, teachers, and other children towards their failures and their successes all contribute to the child's self-esteem.

Low self-esteem and behavioural difficulties

All healthy children frustrate their parents and their teachers by mis-behaving at some time or another. Children with dyslexia are more often likely to do this, mainly as a result of the frustrations caused by not being able to perform as well as the other children. Unfortu-nately, it is all too easy in the heat of the moment for teachers and parents to react to the child's misbehaviour instinctively and often negatively. In so doing, they may inadvertently use words that reduce the child's self-esteem, with the added risk of the misbehaviour escal-ating. It is useful therefore for parents and teachers to be aware of what words to use so that the child's self-esteem is maintained and the risk of the misbehaviour escalating is avoided. The words that are recommended have been the study of the psychologist and educa-tor, Thomas Gordon (1974b). The work of Thomas Gordon on parent and teacher communication is generally recognized as being a classic in the field of self-esteem enhancement. Gordon has shown how it is possible by the judicious use of the right words to enhance self-esteem when talking to children. He has also shown how it is possible to re-duce self-esteem by using the wrong words. This approach is especially advocated when a child is misbehaving.

The Gordon model

The main principle of Gordon's model is the formula: 'I', 'when' and 'because'. Most of us, when feeling irritated or aggressive, will tend to use the word 'you' when addressing the other person. The use of the words I, when, because help to separate the deed from the person carrying out the deed; that is, it separates the offending action from the child who is seen to be misbehaving. Let us suppose that a parent has to chastise a child because of deliberately throwing food around the dinner table. The parent might say the following: '*you* are being a nuisance and a silly child doing that'. This is referred to as using a 'you' message and is construed to be an attack on the child. However, if the Gordon model had been used, the parent might have used the words 'I', 'when', and 'because' as follows, '*I* am cross *when* food is thrown around the table *because* it dirties the table and I have to wash the cloth.'

The reasons for using the words 'I,' 'when' and 'because' are as follows:

> '*I*' – this word allows parents to express their feelings about the behaviour and thus helps to reduce their frustration.
>
> '*When*' – the use of this word describes the offending behaviour and implies that the complaint is not for ever. It is in reference to that specific situation only, so giving the child an opportunity to reform.
>
> '*Because*' – this word gives a reason for the complaint and so shows that the complaint is not merely a whim.

Using this model of communication is considered to be a assertive response rather than an aggressive one. The following two dramatic scenes illustrate the Gordon model:

> **Scene 1**: A display illustrating the *lowering of self-esteem*
> Parent: (*showing anger*) You are a very naughty child and you are being silly.
> Child: (*now feeling afraid*) Sorry.
> Parent: You are an idiot. You never behave properly at the table.
> Child: (*now also feeling angry*) So what!
> Parent: You'll have to grow up one day.
> Child: (*now feeling very upset*) I hate you!
> Parent: (*very angry*) You can now go up to your room and stay there!
>
> **Scene 2**: A display illustrating the *maintenance of self-esteem*
> Parent: When that happens I feel angry because it makes a mess on the tablecloth and I have more work to do washing it.

Child: (*feeling chastised*) Sorry.
Parent: When food is thrown around like that it upsets us all.
Child: (*concerned for the parent*) Sorry, I won't do it again.
Parent: Good. I'm happy to hear it.
Child: I really am sorry I did it.
Parent: I know that you are. I'm sure you will try not to do it
again.

Analysis of Scene 1

Self-esteem was reduced as the child was made to feel stupid and un-wanted. Communication broke down so the situation remained un-resolved.

Analysis of Scene 2

Self-esteem was maintained. The focus of the parent's communication was on the child's behaviour and not on the child's character.

These two dramatic scenes may appear to be somewhat artificial and in real life different words might be used. The use of other words does not matter so long as the words used include 'I', 'when' and 'be-cause'. In using these words the child's self-esteem will be maintained.

Beginning communication with the child by using 'I' in the Gor-don model is more likely to ensure good communication, whereas using the 'you' word will tend to disrupt communication. When com-munication is at its best, it is often said that people are 'on the same wavelength'. They understand and trust each other. Children who feel understood are better able to communicate without being anx-ious over possible criticism. It is essential for the children's self-esteem that teachers and parents establish this kind of communication with children. Dyslexic children are often especially sensitive to criticism. Most will have experienced criticism over their lack of progress in schoolwork, especially if their dyslexia has not been identified.

Enhancing self-esteem

Before discussing how to enhance self-esteem, it is important to be clear exactly what is meant by self-esteem enhancement. Just as there have been many misunderstandings over what is meant by self-esteem, so too are there misunderstandings about enhancing self-esteem. Self-esteem enhancement has probably been subject to even more misunderstandings. For instance, people often think that enhancing self-esteem is all about regularly praising children. This is totally wrong. Self-esteem enhancement means more than praising children. While praise is important, it has to be genuine and appropriate. Children need to be helped to develop a realistic self-image and not a false one. While praise forms a significant role with regard to self-esteem enhancement, it has to be genuine. If children are praised indiscriminately and without justification, they will develop a false idea of themselves. This is known as developing a *faulty self-image*. Praising children without justification can be just as bad for children as no praise at all. Children whose parents give them a faulty self-image will feel valued in the safe family environment. However, as soon as they enter school, they come up against reality and are unprepared for it. They soon begin to experience extreme anxiety, as other people do not relate to them in the same manner as their parents. Eventually this results in the development of low self-esteem. It is far better that parents focus on praising their children's efforts rather than their achievements. This is particularly important to praise effort rather than achievement in the case of children with dyslexia.

Schools today are well aware of the value of focusing on a child's self-esteem and most classrooms provide a self-esteem enhancing environment. Some schools even organize self-esteem enhancement programmes, usually specifically for those children who have been previously identified with low self-esteem.

Although it is recognized that teachers play an important part in developing a child's self-esteem, it is the parents who normally play the greater role. It would be unrealistic for parents to organize in the home the kind of self-esteem enhancement programmes that teachers use at school. However, it is advisable for parents to consider whether their attitudes towards their dyslexic children are positive as illustrated in the short dramatic scene presented in the Gordon model.

The Coopersmith research

It is over 40 years since the mammoth study in the USA, conducted by Stanley Coopersmith (1967), showing how children's self-esteem is affected by parents' self-esteem. The results of this research showed how it is vital for children's self-esteem that parents also have high self-esteem. This research also highlighted the importance of the positive child–parent relationship in promoting self-esteem in the child. Although teachers and parents both have a part to play in children developing self-esteem, in the early years it is the parents who normally play the greater part.

The main conclusion from the Coopersmith research was that parents who demonstrated unconditional love for their children, but who were also able to set limits to their children's behaviour and to have high self-esteem themselves, were more likely to have children with high self-esteem. This conclusion was later supported by the work of Bandura (1970) who showed the powerful effects of modelling. Bandura showed how people who make close relationships with other people have a powerful influence on the other person's behaviour. The corollary is that parents and teachers who have high self-esteem are providing a positive model for the children in their care. This means that the children in their care are also more likely to have high self-esteem.

There is also research evidence to show that the quality of the social interaction between teacher and child is similar to that of the parent–child interaction in its effect on children's self-esteem (Fontana, 1981). In a recent, as yet unpublished study, carried out at the London Institute for Education, the quality of social interaction between parents and children was studied. In this study, children from deprived social backgrounds had higher achievements than children from privileged backgrounds whose parents did not relate to them with sensitivity. Responding with sensitivity means listening to the child. This is discussed in the next section.

Listening to the child

It is clear from both the Coopersmith research and the work of Thomas Gordon that the ability to communicate positively to children is of paramount importance in relation to their self-esteem development and scholastic achievements. The essence of good communication is being able to show the child respect. The precise words suggested in the Gordon model are essential if communicating with a child who is showing difficult behaviour. There is another well-known model of communicating to children recommended by Dinkmeyer and McKay (1976). This is known as *reflective listening*. This model involves listening to children's feelings when they are talking to us. There is a natural tendency in all of us to be too intellectual in a conversation and focus purely on the logic of what is being said to us. Unfortunately, particularly with children, this is often to the detriment of missing interpreting, or ignoring, the child's feelings.

There are usually feelings behind words when child is talking to us. For instance, the child may say, 'I had a rotten day today at school.' A busy parent, not using reflective listening might reply, 'Never mind. Let's go for a walk.' While there may be no harm done with that reply, at the same time an opportunity has been missed to make the child feel understood and supported. A parent using reflective listening might have replied, 'You sound miserable, what happened?' Most children would then express their feelings, begin to communicate more and feel generally more positive. They will feel closer to the parent and therefore be more open to influence from the parent. This approach requires practice but the results are generally worth the effort.

Most children, when first diagnosed as being dyslexic, experience strong emotions. Some will feel relieved believing, for instance, that they now have a justifiable excuse for not being able to spell or to read properly. Other children may react with dismay, or even acute anxiety, believing that the label dyslexia means they have some medical condition. Some children might take the news in their stride with no obvious signs of being concerned unduly. Whatever the children's reactions, it would be safe to say that most of them have some kind of emotional reaction to being informed that they are dyslexic. This is when children would benefit from parents and teachers listening to them, or at least giving them an opportunity to say how they feel about the news. Most parents would probably discuss the diagnosis of dyslexia with their children soon after the assessment. However, it is easy for parents to do all the talking in that kind of situation and miss an opportunity for children to express their feelings about the dyslexia. This is especially so if children do not find it easy to talk about their feelings. Many children need prompting in this respect.

Teachers and parents might like to consider the following guidelines to ensure that they are communicating with children in a self-esteem enhancing way.

Non-verbal behaviour

- Try not to adopt a 'closed manner' when addressing a children, for example, arms folded.
- Always use eye contact when listening or talking to children.
- Try to smile a lot when addressing children.
- Ensure that your voice has a pleasant tone.

Listening skills

- Try not to allow yourself to be distracted when children talk to you.
- Try to 'guess' children's feelings when they are saying something to you.
- Reflect children's feelings back to them when you reply to them.
- Allow children time to finish their comments.

Establishing trust

- Tell children that you trust them to behave well and to make progress.
- Express your own positive feelings to the children about being with them.
- Occasionally reveal your 'non-teaching' side.
- Communicate that you are interested in children's well-being.

Being positive

- Make a point of reading the Gordon model.
- Try to make more positive than negative comments.
- Learn how to change negative comments to positive ones.
- Try to adopt a generally optimistic attitude to life.

Developing expectancies

- Communicate often that you expect the children to make progress.
- Change any negative comments made by children to positive ones.

- Regularly praise the efforts of children.
- Try occasionally to give children responsible tasks.

Summary

There is an association between children's self-esteem, their academic achievements and behavioural problems. Dyslexic children are particularly at risk of developing low self-esteem and unless they are identified early and receive appropriate help, they are also likely to show behavioural problems as well. Children with high self-esteem are more motivated to achieve in schoolwork and also have fewer behavioural problems. Although a child's self-esteem during the early years is influenced mainly by parental attitudes, teachers also play an important part in this process. There is research evidence by Coopersmith and Bandura showing that parents with high self-esteem generally have children with high self-esteem.

There are many misconceptions over the meaning of self-esteem. It is not merely a case of praising children for their achievements. Children need praise but it has to be genuine praise. More importantly, children need first to be valued for themselves irrespective of their achievements. Dyslexic children are almost bound to experience failures at some stage, but it is not failure *per se* that will result in low self-esteem. It is the attitude towards their failures by teachers and parents that will determine their self-esteem. Trial-and-error learning is an inevitable process for most children and especially for dyslexic children. Low self-esteem in children is manifested in different ways according to the child's individual temperament.

Effective methods of communication to maintain self-esteem with children can be learned. Programmes and strategies designed to help parents and teachers enhance their communication skills with children can be found in the work of Gordon (1974) and Dinkmeyer and McKay (1976).

10 Maintaining self-esteem in teachers and parents

Introduction

In their determination to do all they can for their children, parents of children with special needs are notorious for neglecting their own needs. In so doing it is all too easy for them to put their own well-being at risk. Apart from the obvious drain on their physical resources, coping with a child with any kind of disability may also result in adverse psychological stress. If this happens and parents become overstressed, they are in danger of putting their self-esteem at risk. As discussed in the previous chapter, this in turn will affect their child's self-esteem. Overly conscientious teachers are similarly at risk of developing stress and consequently low self-esteem. The main aim of this chapter is to show teachers and parents how to maintain their own self-esteem and to cope with possible stress. Appropriate strategies are outlined for use by teachers and parents, and stress and self-esteem questionnaires outlined for those who may wish to assess their own levels of self-esteem and possible stress.

It is sometimes said that people in today's complex society are more at risk of developing stress and low self-esteem than people who lived in former times. Although dyslexic children's needs are not usually physical, busy parents with families to look after who are also worried about their dyslexic children are also at risk. The busy class teacher who may have a disproportionate number of children requiring special help may also be at risk of developing stress. A second aim of this chapter is help teachers and parents manage possible stress that may result from caring for a child with dyslexia. The chapter begins by defining and explaining what is meant by stress.

Understanding stress

Stress is probably best defined by McGrath (1970) who stated that 'stress is a perceived substantial imbalance between demand and response capability...with perceived undesirable consequences'. This means that stress occurs when people feel they are no longer able to respond properly to the demands made upon them.

There have been countless studies over the years into stress and its effects. Most authors who study these would agree that these are experienced along two dimensions, the physical and the psychological. Stress usually begins with psychological symptoms. What may begin as mental stress eventually spills over into physical stress so that the person not only feels mentally drained but also physically exhausted.

People differ in their capacity to cope with stressful events in their lives. It is probably true to say that most people learn to cope well in the face of many potential stressful events without ever reaching the stage of mental and physical exhaustion. However, everybody has their breaking point and this comes earlier in some than in others. It seems that most people at first deny their stress. However, an emotionally stressful situation does not disappear. The evidence is that stress is a gradual process and cumulative. It occurs when a series of stressful events are piled on top of each other without any of them being resolved. The psychoanalysts would say that if the stressful event has been repressed and is now in the unconscious mind it is still active. Unless each potentially stressful event is acknowledged and recognized for what it is and dealt with, stress can escalate and result in a series of undesirable emotions that ultimately may require the individual to seek professional help.

Degrees of stress

There are degrees of stress. Most people appear to cope well with stressful events in their lives. The majority of teachers and parents who care for dyslexic children probably cope well enough without undue wear and tear. They do not show stress to the extent that that they require professional help. Happily, only a minority of people experience stress that results in mental and physical exhaustion. It is when stress is severe that people may become exhausted and so are likely to need professional help.

Most parents, when informed that their children are dyslexic, will be concerned, but this does not mean that they are necessarily suffering stress as defined above. Their concerns are often easily alleviated after a discussion with their children's teachers and reassurance that their children are receiving appropriate help.

Even though the parents of children who are assessed as being dyslexic may not immediately feel stressed, they may still be at risk. They usually go through a series of mixed emotions, beginning with a feeling of concern. A feeling of disappointment usually follows this initial feeling of concern. This is because most parents identify with their children. When their children fail in something, it feels like it is they who are failing. This is why many parents often become angry at this point or at the very least they feel irritable. Unless they come to terms with their disappointment over discovering they have children who are dyslexic, they are likely to begin to experience some degree of stress. Their stress may be only mild and so would not necessarily result in severe stress. However, even mild stress can be a threat to their self-esteem. Most parents and some teachers who care for children with dyslexia are likely to fall into this category. These are the people who would benefit from the self-help programme outlined in this chapter.

Stress questionnaire

The following questionnaire is a useful tool to help in assessing stress levels.

Mark the following questions: *Yes/No/Don't know.*

During the last week have you

- often felt irritable or bad-tempered for no obvious reason?
- had difficulty in accepting any kind of criticism?
- rarely laughed at anything?
- been worried over not getting some work done?
- found you could not get on with some person?
- not been able to say 'No' to somebody?
- felt strongly unable to lead the life you want to lead?
- felt taken for granted by anybody?

- lay awake at night thinking of problems?
- worried about personal finances?
- not had time for your hobby or your leisure pursuit?
- not been able to take any exercise?
- found it impossible to sit doing nothing?
- eaten, drunk or smoked more than usual?
- experienced headaches or other physical aches?
- found it hard to get out of bed in the morning?
- forgotten to complete an important task?
- felt disappointed in your performance?

Score 2 points for each question answered 'Yes'; 1 point for answering 'Don't Know'; 0 points for answering 'No'.

Key:
0–18   Very relaxed
18–42   You may need to reappraise your goals
42–72   You are stressed and may need to seek help

Self-help strategies

As previously stated, not everybody with signs of stress feels the need to seek professional help. In any case, many people prefer first to try a self-help method of coping in the first instance.

The following strategies are outlined for teachers and parents who do find themselves under stress and may wish to use a self-help method of coping. The strategies presented are research-based and have been used successfully by the author in clinical practice.

The key to stress management lies in learning how to change negative thoughts to more positive ones. When this is done successfully, the negative emotions will eventually change to positive emotions. However, like all things worth achieving, changes will not occur without some effort. It is important that some considerable thought is given to changing the negative emotions combined with regular practice in the associated activities outlined below.

Rational-emotive therapy

There are many self-help methods quoted in the literature but a recommended method with a sound research base is the one known as rational-emotive therapy (RET). The currently popular Cognitive Behavioural Therapy is based on RET. This method owes its origins to the work of Albert Ellis (1979), a New York psychologist and is based on the principle that our emotions are usually caused by our thinking. For instance, we might say, 'That child makes me angry' when, in fact, it is not the child who makes us angry. We make ourselves angry by the way we have interpreted the child's behaviour. Another example might be the way two different people react to the same situation. For instance, the sight of a snake might be experienced with pleasure and regarded as interesting by a person who has worked in a zoo. A person who has never seen a real snake before might react with fear. Whenever a person reacts emotionally to a specific situation, there is always some thinking or interpretation taking place.

There are five stages in a typical RET programme, often referred to as the ABCDE approach. The five stages are:

- identify the *activating* source of the stress (A);
- analyse the *belief* that accompanies the emotion (B);
- identify the emotional *consequences* of the thinking (C);
- logically *dispute* the thinking (D);
- experience the *effect* of the rational solution (E).

The following example of RET is illustrated from a real-life situation involving a teacher under stress:

- *Activating event*   Child is having trouble learning to read.
- *Belief*   'This child will never learn to read. I must be a poor teacher.'
- *Consequence*   'I feel so depressed. I wonder where I have gone wrong.'
- *Disputation*   Where is the evidence that dyslexic children never learn to read?

  'There is no evidence that I am a poor teacher, as other children in my class make progress. Where is the evidence that I have gone wrong somewhere? There is no logical evidence for my statements; therefore I am being irrational. There is evidence that I am a good teacher.'

- *Effect*   'Children usually learn to read once their difficulties have been identified. I must ask for a psychological assessment to identify why this child is having difficulties.'

It is the logical disputation of the thinking that is the essence of the RET approach. It is all too easy to become irrational in our thinking when we become emotional.

Creative visualization and relaxation

The RET strategy should be supplemented by creative visualization and a relaxation exercise. There are two stages to this process and each could be practised separately or in sequence depending on the time available.

Stage one

Relaxation

There are literally hundreds of ways to relax that are listed in the literature. The one listed below is recommended as having been used with success in the author's practice.

- Sit in a comfortable chair.
- Take off your shoes.
- Raise each arm and leg in turn, ensuring they are loose and limp.
- Fix your eyes on a point on the ceiling just above normal eye level.

Close your eyes as soon as it feels you are straining them, allowing your head to fall onto your chest. Think of each of your muscles and joints in turn and relax them, beginning with your toes and working up the body. Legs, sides, shoulders, chest, stomach, neck, face and even your tongue and your mouth should all be relaxed in turn.

Once your body feels perfectly relaxed, observe your breathing and note how it is automatic. The breathing is natural and is outside your conscious control.

- Let 'it' breathe naturally at the rate 'it' wants to, not forcing the breath.
- Observe each breath as it happens, noting how the abdomen rises and falls.
- Say the word 'relax' as each breath is exhaled.

- Continue to breathe and to say 'relax' for at least 10 times until mind and body are perfectly relaxed.

Stage two

Creative visualization

When two events are regularly associated together, the appearance of one will remind us of the other one. This is known as classical conditioning. A stressful event is usually conditioned or associated with anxiety and tension. The aim of this stage is to overturn this conditioning and so decondition the stressful event.

The creative visualization process involves associating the stressful event with relaxation. Stress and relaxation are incompatible feelings. The stressful event is visualized alongside the event that is totally relaxing. It is important to note that more time should be spent on visualizing the relaxing event than time spent on the stressful one. The chosen relaxed event should be a scene where you know you are always relaxed. The scene could be in the past or in the present. This process should be practised regularly at least once a day until relief is experienced and the stressful event has lost its potency. The stages of this process are outlined below:

- Focus on the relaxing scene for five minutes, reliving the sight, the sound and the smell of it.
- Slowly introduce the stressful scene you are trying to cope with. Do not dwell on this scene for more than a few seconds.
- Return to the relaxed scene for another five minutes before focusing for a few *seconds* on the stressful scene again.
- Repeat the procedure until feeling totally relaxed in both scenes, focusing longer now on what should be the less stressful scene.
- Conclude by focusing for a further five minutes on the relaxed scene.

Characteristics of high self-esteem

Some people always appear to be in control of their lives no matter how much stress they may encounter. If subjected to a potentially stressful event, they usually cope without undue wear and tear on their emotions. They always seem to be confident. They are usually popular and make friends easily. This is the behaviour of high self-esteem people. Research has identified the characteristics of high self-esteem people so that it has been possible now to devise specific programmes to help people with low self-esteem change their behaviour. The research has consistently shown that people who have high self-esteem possess three outstanding characteristics. These three characteristics are *empathy, acceptance* and *genuineness*. Each of these terms is explained below.

Empathy

Empathy means being able to feel what other people are feeling and to be able to communicate this to them. This is similar to reflective listening as described in the previous chapter. It implies an ability to listen to other people's feelings as well as to their words. In so doing, the other person not only feels understood but also feels valued and trusted. For instance, a child may say, 'I had a rotten day at school today', and then sit silently, looking miserable. The teacher or the parent who does not empathize might reply, 'That's too bad. Cheer up and we'll have tea.' The teacher or parent who empathizes is more likely to say, 'You sound miserable, it must have been a tough day. Tell me what happened.' The empathetic reply in all probability will produce a further response from the child as the child feels understood. The conversation would continue and the child would in all probability expand on the reason for the original comment and feel supported.

Acceptance

Acceptance means being totally accepting of people without morally judging them. Teachers and parents might legitimately question this statement when it is obvious that some children can be so disruptive that their behaviour cannot be ignored. However, acceptance does not mean that the behaviour is ignored. Acceptance means being able to accept the child even though not accepting the child's difficult behaviour. Sometimes children's behaviour can be so objectionable that it is difficult to relate to them positively. However, it is still possible to accept the child, even if not the behaviour. The key to this attitude is to be able to separate the child who is loved from the undesirable behaviour. This means using the Gordon model demonstrated in the previous chapter.

Genuineness

Genuineness means being able to 'be yourself' and not wear a 'mask', or what Carl Jung called 'a persona'. We all tend to have a degree of reserve but some people hide their real selves with such a strong mask that you never really get to know them. Most teachers and parents are able to be themselves in the safety of their family environment but outside of it some people may feel so insecure that they tend to wear a persona. Some people wear a persona through identifying with their occupations to the extent that they become stereotyped and carry their official role with them outside of their work environment. An example of this is when others refer to a person as being a 'typical policeman' or a 'typical teacher'. They are so lacking in natural spontaneity that they have difficulty in relating to other people on a human level. If this is taken to an extreme, so that they are never able to present the human side of themselves, it will not only be a barrier to communication but it is also mentally unhealthy. It can lead to neurotic illnesses when people are cut off from their instinctual, natural sides. It can most certainly result in low self-esteem. Teachers and parents who do not have this quality of genuineness can make children feel insecure and that is the first step to lowering a child's self-esteem.

Teachers and parents who feel that they need to enhance their self-esteem should reflect on how far they possess the three desirable personal characteristics of empathy, acceptance and genuineness. They might also like to consider engaging in specific activities to practise these qualities. There are several programmes available in the literature that are devised to develop these characteristics, usually designed for small group participation (Lawrence, 2000).

Looking the part – body language

One of the most fascinating topics associated with enhancing self-esteem has been body language or non-verbal behaviour. High self-esteem people are not only confident inside but they usually look confident as well. Their overall body language communicates self-confidence. Their physical stance and facial expressions are relaxed; their tone of voice is well modulated and calm, and they look you straight in the eye when talking to you.

Other people usually react positively to those whose body language conveys self-confidence. Research shows that we tend to judge other people not only by what they say but also by what they look like. It seems that body language is particularly important when first meeting somebody. We make judgements about whether we like another person and whether we trust them on the messages conveyed by their non-verbal behaviour. Moreover, first impressions tend to stick. Experiments have shown, for instance, that students remember what lecturers looked like, what they were wearing and the sound of their voices longer than they remember the contents of a lecture (Argyle, 1994).

The obvious message for people with low self-esteem who wish to change is that they need to consider their body language as well as their psychological factors. There is some evidence that people lacking in confidence will eventually begin to feel confident if they regularly practise adopting a confident manner.

The following questionnaire has been devised to assess self-esteem in adults.

Adult Self-esteem Questionnaire (Lawrence, 2000)

Mark the following questions: *Always/Sometimes/Never*

Are there lots of things about yourself you do not like?

- Do you often worry about things you should have done or said?
- Do you find it hard to get off to sleep at night through worrying?
- Do you often wish you were somebody else?
- Do you try to avoid having to return faulty goods to a shop?
- Do other people often criticize you?
- Are you easily hurt when other people find fault with you?
- Do you try to avoid meetings that could be difficult?

- Do you feel that not many people like you?
- Do you worry a lot about past mistakes you have made?
- Do you tend to give in easily?
- Do you dislike the sound of your own voice?
- Are you ashamed of your background?
- Are you usually anxious when meeting a new person?
- Do you often find it hard to think clearly when in conversation?
- Would you take a drug to help you face a potentially stressful situation?
- Do you dislike your appearance?
- Are other people more popular than you?
- Do you often find it hard to make up your mind about things?

Key: Always = *0*   Sometimes = *1 point*   Never = *2 points*

Scores between 0 and 20 = low self-esteem

Scores between 21 and 30 = average self-esteem

Scores between 31 and 40 = high self-esteem

A Seven-day Self-esteem Maintenance Programme

The Seven-day Self-esteem Maintenance Programme is designed for teachers and parents who may feel the need to maintain their self-esteem. It is recommended that the programme be systematically followed.

Day 1: Make a list of all your positive achievements no matter how small they may seem, for example, putting a plant in the garden, raising a family, cooking dinner, obtaining a qualification.

Day 2: Make a list of all your positive personal qualities, for example, sense of humour, good-natured, helpful to others, courageous.

Day 3: Complete the following sentences:

- The thing I like best about myself is.......................
  ....
- I am most proud of..
  ....

- I am happy when...
  ....
- I get pleasure from.......................................
  ....

Day 4: Recall a situation in which you either said or did something you now regret.

- Talk to yourself positively as if counselling yourself. For example, 'I am not really a bad person. The real me is OK despite what I said (or did). I will forgive myself.'

Day 5: Make plans for a future activity. It does not have to be anything dramatic. It could be simply planting seeds in the garden, taking a holiday or visiting a friend.

Day 6: Indulge yourself. Select a favourite activity, for example, walking, shopping for yourself, reading, having an expensive meal out.

Day 7: Do the relaxation activity outlined earlier in this chapter. When finished, rehearse the following affirmations out loud:

- My past is behind me – my future is before me.
- I am capable of determining my own destiny.
- I am generally a happy person and have a right to be happy.
- People generally like me, as I am a good friend.
- I am a confident person and I like myself.

Summary

Parents of children with any kind of disability or learning difficulty and teachers who have these children in their care are always at risk of developing some degree of emotional stress. Those teachers and parents of dyslexic children would come into this category. There is a recognized association between self-esteem and stress. While most will eventually cope, there are parents and teachers who develop stress symptoms to the extent that it also affects their self-esteem. However, with determination and by following a stress management programme, parents and teachers can reduce their stress and maintain their self-esteem. Practical self-help methods of relaxation and managing stress as well as maintaining self-esteem programme were outlined in this chapter. The completion of the stress and self-esteem questionnaires, also outlined in this chapter, should be helpful in knowing whether these programmes are necessary in any particular case.

11 Society's attitudes towards dyslexia

Introduction

This chapter discusses the particular challenges faced by dyslexic children in everyday living. It also highlights the negative attitudes towards dyslexic people that still exist in some quarters. Also some people question the value of the label 'dyslexia'. Arguments for and against the use of this label are presented in this chapter.

However, it is encouraging to note the many positive developments that have taken place since the official acceptance of dyslexia as a specific learning difficulty. In contrast to former times, most people these days have heard of dyslexia and most teachers in all branches of education are more sensitive today to the needs of the dyslexic student. The introduction of the Special Needs Coordinator (SENCO) into schools has made a tremendous difference to the support and teaching of children with special needs, including children with dyslexia. In addition to the SENCO, an increasing number of teachers today have specialist qualifications in the assessment and teaching of dyslexic children. In the field of higher education, students need no longer be dissuaded from studying for degrees as most universities and colleges now have departments and staff dedicated to providing emotional and practical support for students with dyslexia. The *Special Educational Needs and Disability Act* (SEND) (Department for Education and Science, 2001) was a boost in that direction. As a result of the SEND Act all educational institutions in the UK are now empowered to provide services to support students with dyslexia. In higher education, dyslexic students are now eligible to apply for financial assistance to purchase equipment such as dictaphones to record lectures, and computers to assist them in writing essays.

It has been asserted by some authors that dyslexic children are unusually gifted and ultimately achieve fame and fortune as a result. This viewpoint and some myths regarding dyslexia are examined in this chapter. The need for more recognition of the concept of dyslexia is asserted in this chapter, referring to the role that parent bodies have played over the years in publicizing the needs of dyslexic children. The chapter begins by discussing why some people continue to question the existence of dyslexia.

The challenge of dyslexia

Despite the encouraging developments that have taken place in the understanding of the origins and management of dyslexia, there are still some people who question the existence of dyslexia. Regardless of the persuasive research evidence that has accumulated over the last couple of decades, there is still a minority that appear to be unaware of what is meant by dyslexia and fail to appreciate the frustrations experienced by people with dyslexia.

Ignorance in society generally regarding the topic of dyslexia is perhaps the greatest challenge facing people with dyslexia. It is not uncommon, for instance, for people to equate dyslexia with a lack of intelligence. There is little doubt of the urgent need for more education about the meaning of dyslexia in order to combat the widespread ignorance of this specific learning difficulty. It continues to disappoint that so many people still do not fully understand dyslexia or appreciate the distress that can be caused by it. This can only compound the inevitable difficulties that dyslexic children and dyslexic adults have to face in their everyday lives.

Perhaps one of the reasons why there is so much of a lack of understanding of dyslexia is that much of the interesting research findings seems to remain in the professional journals and does not reach the popular press.

A further possible reason for a lack of knowledge regarding dyslexia is that dyslexia cannot be observed directly. In the case of most physical disabilities, the actual condition can be seen. Dyslexia, on the other hand, unlike a physical disability, cannot be observed directly. A parallel with this would be the child with a hearing loss. A hearing loss is an example of another hidden difficulty. People often become irritated when a person appears not to hear them and does not quickly respond to them. Dyslexic children often encounter a similar lack of understanding. As people do not easily see evidence of dyslexia, people do not always make allowances for it.

It is a common misapprehension that dyslexia is concerned only with literacy difficulties. Dyslexia is wider than difficulties with reading. Dyslexia affects not only literacy skills but also everyday living. Although literacy difficulties are probably the dyslexic children's most common problem, their dyslexia also presents them with other challenges. The underlying deficits that affect their learning of literacy skills may also affect their social relationships. They may easily forget instructions. This weakness in working memory tends to cause others to become irritated and impatient with them. Even when a child is known to be dyslexic, it is not easy for other people to appreciate the distress that a weakness in working memory can cause. Wherever dyslexic children have to perform tasks that are dependent on working memory, they will be at a disadvantage. Their working memory easily becomes overloaded and so dyslexic children are likely to ask for instructions to be repeated. They also often have a problem with general organization so they are likely also to have difficulty with tasks such as keeping their rooms tidy. With patience and understanding, most dyslexic children learn to cope. However, if irritation is the immediate reaction from other people, then dyslexic children are going to experience further frustrations as well as the risk of their self-esteem being reduced.

Public displays of dyslexia

A public display of any kind of personal weakness is potentially stressful and a threat to the self-esteem. In modern life there are many situations where people are expected to perform in view of other people. Dyslexic children face many challenges outside school where their dyslexia can be a problem. One example of this is when older dyslexic children go shopping. They are often slow to process information and so are likely to be slow to count out the correct money. This can cause children acute embarrassment at a checkout, for instance, when other people see them being unusually slow.

Recent advances in technology and electronics in this digital age have placed extra demands on most people. New electronic gadgets and more complicated machines are increasingly being invented. For example, many mobile phones are capable of performing other functions that also need to be learned. Today's mobile phone can also carry out the functions of a camera and a computer. Adolescents have always had a need to be part of their group so it is not surprising that most adolescents own one of these gadgets. The child with dyslexia would be no exception to this. However, the necessary multiple operation of the mobile phone can present the dyslexic child with many problems. Remembering the precise details of how to operate these new innovations presents a particular challenge, as well as having to learn to have to coordinate their manual operation.

Some myths about dyslexia

Research into dyslexia and its antecedents is still in its infancy, compared with the research into other topics in psychology. There are still many questions waiting to be answered. Inevitably, therefore, statements are sometimes made about dyslexia that are not based on scientific evidence. One example of this is the statement that people with dyslexia have special talents that will enable them to achieve greatness in their chosen field. While there is some evidence that creative abilities are especially strong in dyslexic children, there is no reliable evidence to date to show that all dyslexic children will inevitably be creative. It is true to say that there are numerous examples of people with dyslexia who have achieved creative heights in their chosen fields. These include famous scientists, actors, sports people and successful heads of business. In an attempt to encourage children with dyslexia, attention is sometimes drawn in the literature to these famous people who are dyslexic. While this is a laudable aim, this kind of encouragement needs to be done sensitively as it may easily backfire and place dyslexic children under pressure to achieve the same. In fact, there is no research to date to show that people with dyslexia achieve any higher than those without dyslexia. Very few people, including those without dyslexia, achieve fame and success to the extent of those usually held up as models. People with dyslexia often do achieve greatness, but when they do, the chances are that it will have been despite their dyslexia and not because of it. There is nothing wrong in bringing the names of these famous dyslexic people to the attention of children with dyslexia provided this point is understood. After all, there are many dyslexic people who have achieved fame and fortune who are excellent role models. The successful people should be discussed with dyslexic children as examples of how dyslexia need not be a barrier to success and not presented to them as models they should be expected to emulate.

Some authors have claimed that children with dyslexia are particularly suited to becoming successful engineers when they become adults. While this may be the case among a selected sample, there is no research evidence to show that people with dyslexia make better engineers than those without dyslexia. The same conclusions have been made regarding the dyslexic person's ability to use computers. There is no reliable evidence to show that dyslexic people are any better at using computers than those without dyslexia. This myth may have arisen because people with dyslexia tend, on the whole, to choose college practical courses rather than academic courses.

One particular myth that needs to be dispelled is that dyslexia is a condition of childhood only. Although all the early research and interest in dyslexia focused on children with dyslexia, there is now ample evidence to show that the problem continues into adulthood albeit sometimes in very different ways. Societal demands placed upon the adult are inevitably wider than those placed upon the child.

Arguments against using the label 'dyslexia'

Many parents worry about the use of the word dyslexia. It could be argued that applying a 'label' to any kind of disability does a disservice to the child. The labelling of children in the field of special education has been a controversial topic for some years now. It is over 30 years since the government-sponsored *Warnock Report* (1978) recommended the abolition of labels in special education and the arguments against labelling still rage today. It could be argued that there are disadvantages against using the label of dyslexia. First, if a label is used to describe a child with any kind of disability, there is a tendency to think that all children with the same label have exactly the same difficulties. This is usually far from the case. As noted earlier in this book, dyslexia can take many forms and also there are different degrees of it. It is most unlikely that two children diagnosed as being dyslexic will demonstrate exactly the same behaviour and to the same degree. They are likely to be different both in terms of the degree and type of their learning difficulty, as well as in their personalities. This is why some educationalists have preferred the phrase *children with a specific learning difficulty* to the label *dyslexia.*

Another argument that is sometimes used against the use of a label to describe a disability is that people tend to perceive the label first and to perceive the child second. It is a fact that there is a tendency in some quarters to talk of 'dyslexics', rather than children who have dyslexia. This may mean of course that the disability might come to mind first rather than the child with all the prejudices that can bring.

A further argument against using labels to describe any kind of disability is that labels can become part of a person's self-concept and so there is always the danger of the self-fulfilling prophecy occurring. In other words, children who are labelled dyslexic may have a tendency to behave in terms of their label. Children labelled as being dyslexic know that they are considered to have a learning difficulty. They may then easily be influenced by the label to believe that they will always have difficulty with schoolwork. This may mean that perhaps they will think that it is not worth making an effort. It has been known for some children with dyslexia to assert, 'I prefer to do other things like art because I am dyslexic and cannot be expected to read and spell.' They believed that they lacked the ability to make progress in literacy skills and so they made very little effort to improve their attainments.

These may seem to be strong arguments against using the label dyslexia. However, while there may be some disadvantages in using a label, there are distinct advantages.

Advantages of using the label dyslexia

First, the use of a label makes for easier communication. It seems to be a natural human phenomenon to want to classify events and concepts and then to apply labels to them. For instance, we find the label 'furniture store' a useful term to describe a place where chairs, tables, beds, and so on are sold. Furniture is an umbrella term beneath which there are countless other objects. Using the label 'furniture' avoids the need to list all the items when discussing the kind of place that sells these articles. Dyslexia is also an umbrella term beneath which there is a list of different behaviours. So the use of the label 'dyslexia' should present no problems just as long as it is understood that it may describe a variety of behaviours. Only a further investigation can determine its precise manifestations, as every child is different.

The disadvantages of using the label need not apply as long as people are aware that the term can comprise a number of difficulties. Note the phrase 'as long as people are aware'. This is the heart of the matter. If people were to fully understand the concept of dyslexia and its effects, the arguments against using the label of dyslexia would no longer be valid. Above all, it should be explained that dyslexia does not necessarily mean that the child is going to be handicapped.

A more useful approach than to argue over whether to use the label dyslexia would be to give dyslexia more publicity so that people become more familiar with the topic and know what it means. As long as people are confused about the term dyslexia, it remains a challenge to all those involved in the fields of special education and educational administration to educate the public regarding the concept of dyslexia. There is an urgent need to do this, not only in the interests of educating the public, but also in order to support dyslexic children, many of whom regularly suffer through ignorance of their disability.

Final thoughts on dyslexia

Dyslexia, over recent years, has been so well researched that the old arguments about whether the condition exists have finally been laid to rest. There is now ample research evidence to demonstrate the existence of an identifiable group of both children and adults who have continued difficulties with literacy skills despite having had appropriate learning experiences. Although there are some arguments against labelling, on the whole it would seem more useful to describe these difficulties with the label dyslexia.

There is also evidence for dyslexia being of biological and genetic origin. There is evidence now for an association between neurological deficits and dyslexia. Although an association has been established, whether neurological deficits directly cause dyslexia or an effect of the dyslexia has still to be formally established. It is hoped that further research will provide the answer to this.

Even among those who appear to understand dyslexia there is sometimes a reluctance to do anything about it. For instance, despite the fact that dyslexia is now recognized in most schools as an official category of disability, there is still no requirement in schools to employ a teacher who is specially qualified in the teaching of dyslexic children. Although it is encouraging that there is government money made available to schools for the management of children with specific learning difficulties, there is no requirement that schools should spend it on children with dyslexia. The specific allocation of money for learning difficulties provision is still up to the individual schools. There is nothing to prevent a head teacher from using the funds to provide a specialist teacher in the teaching of other kinds of learning difficulty. Unfortunately, this is more than likely to happen as long as there are teachers who are still unaware or unconvinced of the existence of dyslexia as a specific learning difficulty.

It is encouraging to note the increase in the number of specialist teachers who are doing stalwart work with dyslexic children. Although without doubt teachers provide the main source of help, parents also have a part to play. It remains a fact that parents usually know their children best. There may be times when parents suspect that their children could be dyslexic even though the children's schools have not mentioned the possibility. Parents should not be afraid to approach the schools if this occurs. This can then lead to an investigation and appropriate help given. Occasionally, however, schools may be reluctant to accept that children have dyslexia. This can be distressing for parents. Fortunately, this state of affairs is becoming less frequent as dyslexia research receives more publicity. However, there are still isolated cases where this happens. Faced with these circumstances, it can be frustrating for parents and it is understandable if concerned parents have a dispute with teachers over this. It is essential if this happens that parents continue to maintain positive communications with teachers. After all, both teachers and parents generally have the children's best interests at heart. A rational discussion with teachers is the best approach, with parents giving reasons why they suspect dyslexia in their children. If teachers still refuse to consider that the children may be dyslexic, despite a rational account from the parents, the next step would be to request an official opinion from an educational psychologist or a teacher especially qualified in the assessment of dyslexia.

As discussed in Chapter 10, it is all too easy for some parents to become stressed when their children are diagnosed as being dyslexic. When this happens, they are in danger of becoming obsessed with their children's dyslexia, as well as being stressed by it. Many parents like this opt to try to teach their children themselves. This should be resisted. It is at times like this that efforts have to be made to keep the topic of dyslexia in proportion. The teaching of literacy skills is rightly the province of the class teacher and parents should try to maintain positive communications with the school. Teachers may need to reassure parents that the school recognizes children's needs and is organizing all of the academic support required.

Under these circumstances, teachers may ask parents to help their children at home. Parents can sometimes supplement the work of the teacher by things such as giving their children practice in the mechanics of reading and also with the development of other skills such as listening skills and phonological awareness. Most teachers would be only too happy to guide parents on how to help their children develop these skills at home. If this is done, it should always be done sensitively and in a fun atmosphere. It is not a good idea for parents to duplicate the school environment in the home. Above all, children need to know that their home is the place where they can feel safe and relaxed after a hard day's work in school, without being made to feel pressure to do more work.

It is sometimes easy for parents to become dispirited in the face of the general ignorance in society and in some schools that still exists over dyslexia. And they can be forgiven for sometimes feeling impotent when faced with the reluctance in some quarters to accept that their child is dyslexic. However, parents of dyslexic children need not feel dismayed. The history of dyslexia shows how parents have often been instrumental in changing public attitudes towards dyslexia. Pressure from parents has often influenced official government policy. One example of this is the efforts of parents that saw the establishment of the *British Dyslexia Association* and the *British Dyslexia Institute,* recently renamed *Dyslexia Action.* These institutions have been responsible not only for promoting the interests of dyslexic children and supporting parents but they have also been instrumental in the establishment of training courses for teachers of dyslexic children. Parents of dyslexic children continue to have an important role to play in the publicizing of dyslexia. Political pressure still needs to be applied by parents in order to improve the provision for dyslexic children in many of our schools.

Finally, it is the positive *attitude* that children develop towards their dyslexia that will ultimately determine their progress. Teachers and parents need to be aware of the importance of helping dyslexic children develop this positive attitude, not only towards their dyslexia but also towards themselves. Children with dyslexia who are helped to focus on their strengths and not their weaknesses are more likely to maintain their self-esteem and so remain motivated to learn. It is up to parents, as well as teachers, to communicate to dyslexic children that they do have the capacity to succeed. One of the greatest strengths anybody can possess is self-belief. Provided dyslexic children are given appropriate help and develop high self-esteem, there need be no limit to their achievements.

Summary

This chapter focused on the need for more education in society regarding the concept of dyslexia. The arguments encountered regarding the use of labels were discussed with particular reference to the advantages and disadvantages of using the label dyslexia. After consideration of the arguments for and against labelling, it is concluded that the label dyslexia is preferred. Children with dyslexia should not regard the label as a handicap. They should be reminded by teachers and parents that there is evidence for dyslexic people achieving at all levels of society despite their dyslexia. There is some evidence that many dyslexic children are particularly creative. There are some famous dyslexic adults who have achieved highly in creative occupations. It is not altogether clear, however, whether their successes are products of their dyslexia or due to other factors. It is important, therefore, that dyslexic children are not put under undue pressure to achieve simply because there are some dyslexic people who have achieved unusual success in society as adults.

In conclusion, although dyslexia is now formally recognized in educational circles, there seems to be a continued need for public education programmes to increase awareness of dyslexia in society generally. It has been mainly through the dedication and perseverance of parents that dyslexia is now a recognized learning difficulty. It is to be hoped that parents of dyslexic children will continue to lobby the appropriate authorities for improved facilities in schools and for more provision for dyslexic children.

It should be emphasized that despite their dyslexia, there need be no limit to dyslexic children's ultimate achievements provided they are given appropriate help and their self-esteem is maintained.

Appendix I

Scotopic Sensitivity Screening Questionnaire

When reading does the child:

1. skip words or sentences?
2. often lose his or her place?
3. misread words?
4. repeat or reread lines?
5. often insert words from the line above or the line below?
6. avoid reading if possible?
7. dislike reading aloud?
8. read very slowly?
9. sometimes reverse letters or words?
10. prefer to read in a dim light?
11. find that words sometimes become blurred or appear to change shape?
12. often need to use a finger as a marker?
13. find that his or her eyes often become watery or red?
14. often get headaches after reading?
15. show that it is an effort to keep his or her eyes on the line?
16. often need to blink when reading?

(Reproduced and amended by permission of Karen Truscott, HMS Raleigh)

Appendix II

A Checklist for Dyslexia

Does the child:

- confuse left and right?
- try to avoid reading books?
- have a problem remembering verbal instructions?
- find it hard to do arithmetical sums in his or her head?
- have a problem with following directions?
- have a problem remembering verbal instructions?
- find it hard to say the correct words in a conversation?
- make lots of spelling mistakes?
- often mispronounce words?
- find it hard to keep to an agreed time?
- forget appointments?
- miss out words when writing essays or letters?
- find it hard to remember nursery rhymes?
- often seems not to hear you when speaking?
- find it hard to keep his or her room tidy?
- find it hard to catch a ball?
- find it hard to balance on one leg and/or walk along a fence or a wall?
- find it hard to concentrate for long on any task?
- appear to lack confidence in most situations?
- become easily embarrassed?

Appendix III

Screening Checklist for ADHD

Does the child:

1. often feel compelled to move around a room?
2. often fidget with his or her hands and/or his or her limbs?
3. find it hard to sit down for long without having to keep moving?
4. find it hard to concentrate on a TV programme?
5. find it hard to listen to other people without interrupting them?
6. find it difficult to wait his or her turn?
7. often talk incessantly?
8. find it easy to be distracted by outside events when watching TV?
9. find it hard to sit and listen to somebody reading to him or her?
10. find it hard to concentrate for more than few seconds on drawing or crayoning?

If more than 5 items are rated 'Yes' there would be need for further investigation

Glossary

Attention deficit hyperactivity disorder (ADHD) is a personality disorder that interferes with prolonged concentration and is manifested through restless behaviour.

Binocular instability refers to a physiological condition where eye movements tend to move from right to left.

Cognitive functioning refers to behaviour that is concerned with thinking, perceiving and processing information, including intelligent behaviour.

Dyscalculia is a difficulty with mathematics that is manifested by an inability to process mathematical symbols.

Dyslexia is a specific learning difficulty of neurological and biological origin that is characterized by a significant discrepancy between measures of working memory and reasoning ability that may be manifested through weaknesses in a variety of educational attainments particularly in literacy skills, as well as in everyday tasks.

Dyspraxia is a term used to describe a weakness in motor coordination.

Intelligence refers to reasoning and problem-solving ability in both verbal and non-verbal spheres.

Lateral confusion is the term given to describe people who tend to confuse left from right.

Learning style refers to a preferred way of problem solving.

Magnetic resonance imaging is a term used to describe a method of measuring the blood flow in the brain to identify areas activated by different stimuli.

Magnocells are neurones in the brain that monitor sensory and motor activities and are thought to influence the synchronization of events.

Non-cognitive factors refer to behaviour concerned with personality and emotions and includes such factors as self-esteem, locus of control and motivation.

Norms are the test scores of a previously obtained sample of people. They are used to compare an individual's score with the average score obtained by others of the same age on that particular test.

Phonemes are the sounds associated with letters.

Phonological refers to the study of letter sounds.

Scotopic sensitivity is a sensitivity to certain light frequencies that causes printed material to become blurred and often appears to move.

Statistical significance is a statistical term that refers to the extent to which a test score, or a discrepancy between two test scores, could have arisen by chance.

Strephosymbolia is a term first used by Dr Orton to describe the reversal of letters when writing.

Word blindness is a term introduced by Dr James Hinshelwood to describe difficulties with reading and spelling. This term has generally been substituted by the term dyslexia.

Working memory refers to the act of recalling information and simultaneously processing it, for example, the calculation of mental arithmetic sums presented orally.

Bibliography

Alloway, T.P. (2001) *Automated Working Memory*. London: Assessment Harcourt.

Alloway, T.P. (2007) *Automated Working Memory Assessment*. London: Harcourt.

Argyle, M. (1994) *The Psychology of Interpersonal Behaviour*. Harmondsworth: Penguin.

Armstrong, T. (1994) *Multiple Intelligences in the Classroom*. Cloverdale, CA: Association for Supervision and Curriculum Development.

Armstrong, T. (1999) *Multiple Intelligences in the Classroom*. Alexandria, VA: Association for Supervision and Curriculum Development.

Baddeley, A.D. (1986) *Working Memory*. Oxford: Clarendon Press.

Bandura, A. (1970) *Principles of Behaviour Modification*. London: Holt, Rinehart & Winston.

Best, M. and Demb, J.B. (1999) Normal planum temporale symmetry in dyslexics with magnocellular pathway deficit, *Neuro Report*, 10: 607–12.

Bishop, D.V. (2007) Curing dyslexia and ADHD by training motor coordination: miracle or myth? *Journal of Paediatrics and Child Health*, 43: 653–5.

Blachman, B. (ed.) (1997) *Foundations of Reading Acquisition and Dyslexia*. Hove: Lawrence Erlbaum Associates Ltd.

Borsting, E. (1996) The presence of magno-cellular defects depends on the type of dyslexia, *Vision Research*, 36: 1047–53.

Bruner, J., Goodwin, J. and Austin, G. (1960) *A Study of Thinking*. New York: Wiley.

Carter, P. (1998) *Mapping the Mind*. London. Weidenfeld & Nicolson.

Chinn, D.J. and Ashcroft, R. (1997) *Mathematics for Dyslexics: A Teaching Handbook*. London: Whurr.

Combley M. (2000) *Hickey Multisensory Language Course*. London: Whurr.

Coopersmith, S. (1967) *The Antecedents of Self-esteem*. San Francisco, CA: Freeman Press.

Davis, R.D. and Braun E.M. (2003) *The Gift of Dyslexia: Why Some of the Brightest People Can't Read and How They Might Learn*. Penguin Putnam/Perigee Books. Berkeley, CA: Berkeley Publishing.

Dennison, P. (1981) *Switching ON*. Ventura, CA: International Educational Kinesology Foundation.

Department for Education and Employment (DFEE) (1994) *Code of Practice on the Identification and Assessment of Educational Needs*. London: HMSO.

Department of Education and Science (2001) *Special Education Needs and Disability Act*. London: HMSO.

Dinkmeyer, D. and Meyer, G.D. (1976) *Systematic Training for Effective Parenting*. Minnesota: American Guidance Service.

Doman, G. and Delacato, C. (1968) Doman-Delacato philosophy, *Human Potential*, 1: 112–16.

Dore, W. (2006) *Dyslexia: The Miracle Cure*. London: Blake.

Dunn, R. (2000) Learning styles, theory, research and practice, *National Forum of Applied Educational Research Journal*, 13(1): 3–22.

Elliot, C. (1997) *British Ability Scales*. Windsor: NFER.

Ellis, A. (1979) *Theoretical and Empirical Foundations of Rational Emotive Therapy*. Monterey, CA: Brooks/Cole.

Evans, B. (2001) *Dyslexia and Vision*. London: Whurr.

Eysenck, H. (1980) *Psychology is About People*. Harmondsworth: Penguin.

Fagerheim, T. (1999) A new gene (DYX3) for dyslexia is located on chromosome 2, *Journal of Medical Genetics*, 36: 664–9.

Fawcett, A. and Nicolson, R. (2004) *Dyslexia Adult Screening Test*. London: Psychological Corporation.

Fisher, S. and Smith, S. (2001) Progress towards the identification of genes influencing developmental dyslexia, in A.J. Fawcett (ed.) *Dyslexia: Theory and Good Practice*. London: Whurr.

Fontana, D. (1981) *Psychology for Teachers*. London: Macmillan Press.

Frederickson, N., Frith, V. and Reason, R. (1997) *Phonological Assessment Battery*. Slough: National Foundation for Educational Research.

Freed, J. (1997) *Right-brained Children in a Left-brained World*. Denver: Simon & Schuster.

Frith, V. (1999) Paradoxes in the definition of dyslexia, *Dyslexia*, 5(4): 192–214.

Galaburda, A. (1989) Ordinary and extraordinary brain development in anatomical variations and developmental dyslexia, *Annals of Dyslexia*, 39: 67–80.

Galton, F. (1869) *Hereditary Genius: An Enquiry into its Laws and Consequences*. New York: Horizon.

Gardner, H. (1983) *Frames of Mind: The Theory of Multiple Intelligences*. New York: Harper & Row.

Gardner, H. (2000) *Intelligence Reframed: Multiple Intelligences for the 21st Century*. New York: Basic Books.

Garzia, R. (1993) Optometric factors in reading disability, in D.M. Willows (ed.) *Visual Processes in Reading and Reading Disabilities*, Mahwah, New Jersey: Lawrence Earlbaum Associates, Inc.

Gathercole, S.E. (2008) Working memory in the classroom, *The Psychologist*, 21(5): 382–5.

Gathercole, S.E. and Baddeley, A.D. (1990) Phonological deficits in language disordered children: is there a causal connection? *Journal of Memory and Language*, 29: 336–60.

Gathercole, S.E. and Baddeley, A.E. (1993) *Working Memory and Language*. Hove, UK: Erlbaum Associates Ltd.

Geschwind, N. and Behan, P.O. (1982) Left-handedness: association with immune disease, migraine, and developmental learning disorder. *Proceedings of the National Academy for Science*, USA.

Geschwind, N. and Galaburda, A. (1985) Cerebral lateralisation–biological mechanisms, associations and pathology: a hypothesis and a programme for research, *Archives of Neurology*, 42: 428–59.

Gillingham, A. and Stillman, B. (1936) *Remedial Work for Reading, Spelling, and Penmanship*. New York: Hackett and Wilhelms.

Good, T.L. and Brophy J.E. (1984) *Looking in Classrooms*. New York: Harper & Row.

Goodman, G. and Poillion, M.J. (1992) ADD: acronym for any dysfunction or difficulty, *Journal of Special Education*, 26: 37–56.

Gordon, T. (1974a) *Parent Effectiveness Training*. New York: Wyden.

Gordon, T. (1974b) *Teacher Effectiveness Training*. New York: Wyden.

Goswami, U. (1991) Recent work on reading and spelling development, in M. Snowling and M.E. Thompson (eds) *Dyslexia: Integrating Theory and Practice*. Chichester: Wiley.

Goulandris, N. and Snowling, M. (1991) Visual memory deficits: a plausible cause of developmental dyslexia. Evidence from a single case study, *Cognitive Neuropsychology*, 8: 1127–54.

Grigorenko, E.L. (1997) Susceptibility loci for distinct components of developmental dyslexia on chromosomes 6 and 15, *The American Journal of Human Genetics*, 60: 27–39.

Hampshire, S. (1982) *Susan's Story*. New York: St. Martin's Press.

Hargreaves, D.H. (1972) *Interpersonal Relations in Education*. London: Routledge.

Harris, A.J. (1979) Lateral dominance and reading disability, *Journal of Learning Disabilities*, 12(5): 337–43.

Henderson, A. (2000) *Maths for the Dyslexic: A Practical Guide*. London: Fulton.

Herbert, M.R., Deutsch, C.K., Kennedy, D., Bakardjier, A., Makris, N. and Caviness, V. (2005) Brain asymmetries in autism and language disorders, *Brain*, 128(1): 213–26.

Hinshelwood, J. (1900) Congenital word-blindness, *Lancet*, 1: 1506–8.

Irlen, H. (1991) *Reading by Colors*. New York: Avery Group.

Johnston, R.S. (1998) The case for orthographic knowledge, *Journal of Research in Reading*, 21(3): 195–200.

Kavale, K.A. and Forness, S.R. (1996) Social skills deficits and learning disabilities: a meta-analysis, *Journal of Learning Disabilities*, 29(3): 236–7.

Kirby, A. and Drews, S. (2003) *Guide to Dyspraxia and Developmental Disorders*. London: David Fulton.

Kosk, L. (1974) Developmental dyscalculia, *Journal of Learning Disabilities*, 7: 164–77.

Lawrence, D. (1999) *Teaching with Confidence: A Guide to Enhancing Teacher Self-esteem*. London: Sage Publications.

Lawrence, D. (2000) *Building Self-esteem with Adult Learners*. London: Sage Publications.

Lawrence, D. (2006) *Enhancing Self-esteem in the Classroom*, 3rd edn. London: Sage Publications.

Lazear, D. (1994) *Seven Pathways of Learning: Teaching Students and Parents about Multiple Intelligences*. Tucson, AZ: Zephyr Press.

Lazear, D. (1999) *Eight Ways of Knowing: Teaching for Multiple Intelligences*. Arlington Heights IL: SkyLight Professional Development.

McGrath, J.E. (1970) *Social and Psychological Factors in Stress*. New York: Holt, Reinhart & Winston.

McLoughlin, D., Fitzgibbon, G. and Young, V. (1994) *Adult Dyslexia: Assessment, Counselling and Training*. London: Whurr.

McLoughlin, D., Leather, C. and Stringer, P. (2002) *The Adult Dyslexic: Interventions and Outcomes*. London: Whurr.

Meares, O. (1980) Figure/ground brightess, and reading disabilities, *Visible Language*, 14: 13–29.

Miles, T.R. (1982) *The Bangor Dyslexia Test*. Wisbech: Learning Development Aids.

Miles, T.R. (1996) Do dyslexic children have IQs? *Dyslexia*, 2(3): 175–8.

Miles, T.R. and Miles E. (1999) *Dyslexia: 100 Years On*, 2nd edn. Milton Keynes: Open University Press.

Mortimore, T. (2003) *Dyslexia and Learning Style: A Practitioner's Handbook*. London: Whurr.

Mortimore, T. (2005) Dyslexia and learning style: a note of caution, *British Journal of Special Education*, 32(3): 145–9.

Muter, V., Hume, C. and Snowling, M. (1997) *Phonological Abilities Test*. London: The Psychological Corporation.

Naidoo, S. (1972) *Specific Dyslexia*. London: Invalid Children's Aid Association.

Neale, M. (1970) *Analysis of Reading Ability*. London: Macmillan.

Nicolson, R. and Fawcett, A. (1995) Dyslexia is more than a phonological disability, *Dyslexia: An International Journal of Research and Practice*, 1: 19–37.

Nicolson, R. and Fawcett, A.J. (1996) *The Dyslexia Early Screening Test.* London: Psychological Corporation.

Nicolson, R. and Fawcett, A. (1999) Automaticity: a new framework for dyslexia research? *Cognition,* 30: 159–82.

Nicolson, R. and Fawcett, A. (2006) Do cerebellar deficits underlie physiological problems in dyslexia? *Developmental Science,* 9(3): 259–62.

Nicolson, R., Fawcett, A. and Baddeley, A. (1992) *Working Memory and Dyslexia.* London: Whurr.

Olson, R.K., Wise, B., Connors, F., Rack, J. and Fulker, D. (1989) Specific deficits in component reading and language skills: genetic and environmental influences, *Journal of Learning Disabilities,* 22: 339–48.

Orton, S.T. (1925) Word blindness in school children, *Archives of Neurology and Psychiatry,* 14: 581–615.

Papagno, C., Valentine, T. and Baddeley, A.D. (1991) Phonological short-term memory and foreign language vocabulary learning, *Journal of Memory and Language,* 30: 331–47.

Perfetti, C.A. (1985) *Reading Ability.* New York: Oxford University Press.

Pickering, S. (2000) Working memory and dyslexia, in T. Mortimore (2003) *Dyslexia and Learning Style: A Practitioner's Handbook.* London: Whurr.

Pickering, S.J. and Gathercole, S.E. (2001) *The Working Memory Test Battery for Children.* London: Harcourt.

Portwood, M. (2002) School-based trials of fatty acid supplements. Paper presented at the Durham County Council Education Conference, June.

Pumphrey, P.D. (1996) *Specific Developmental Dyslexia: Basics to Back?* Leicester: The Education Section of the British Psychological Society.

Rack, J.P. (1994) Dyslexia: the phonological deficit hypothesis, in A. Fawcett and R. Nicolson (eds.) *Dyslexia in Children: Multi-disciplinary Perspectives.* London: Harvester Wheatsheaf.

Ramos, F., Pidgeon, E. and Frith, U. (2003) The relationship between motor control and phonology in dyslexic children, *Journal of Child Psychology and Psychiatry,* 44(5): 712–22.

Raven, J.C. (1998) *Standard Progressive Matrices.* Oxford: Oxford Psychologists.

Reid, G. (2003) *Dyslexia: A Practitioner's Handbook,* 3rd edn. London: Wiley Blackwell.

Reynolds, D., Nicolson, R. and Hamblyn, H. (2003) Evaluation of an exercise-based treatment for children with reading difficulties, *Dyslexia,* 9(2): 127–33.

Rochelle, K.S.H. and Talcott, J.B. (2006) Impaired balance in developmental dyslexia? A meta analysis of the existing evidence, *Journal of Child Psychology and Psychiatry,* 47(11): 1159–66.

Rosenthal, R. and Jacobson, L. (1968) *Pygmalion in the Classroom: Teacher Expectations and Pupil's Intellectual Develoment*. New York: Holt, Rinehart & Winston.

Rotter, J.B. (1954) *Social Learning and Clinical Psychology*. Engelwood Cliffs, NJ: Prentice Hall.

Rutter, M. and Yule, W. (1975) The concept of specific reading retardation, *Journal of Child Psychology and Psychiatry*, 16: 181–97.

Scarborough, H.S. (1990) Very early language deficits in children, *Child Development*, 61: 1728–43.

Schultz, R.T., Shaywitz, S.E. et al. (1994) Brain morphology in normal and dyslexic children: the influence of sex and age, *Annals of Neurology*, 35: 732–42.

Seligman, M. (1991) *Learned Optimism*. London: Random House.

Shalev, R.S., Manor, O., Karam, B. and Ayali, M. (2001) Developmental dyscalculia is a familial learning disability, *Journal of Learning Disabilities*, 34: 1–59.

Shaywitz, S.E. (1996) Dyslexia, *Scientific American*, November: 98–104.

Silverman, L.K. (2004) *Upside-down Brilliance: The Visual–Spatial Learner*. Denver, CO: DeLeon.

Smith, L. and Wilkins, A. (2007) How many colours are necessary to increase the reading speed of children with word stress?: a comparison of two systems, *Journal of Reading Research*, 30(3): 332–93.

Snowling, M.J. (1995) Phonological processing and developmental dyslexia, *Journal of Reasearch in Reading*, 18: 132–8.

Snowling, M. (2000) *Dyslexia*, 2nd edn. Oxford: Blackwell.

Snowling, M.J. (2001) *Dyslexia*. Oxford: Blackwell.

Snowling, M. and Stackhouse, J. (1996) *Dyslexia, Speech and Language*. London: Whurr.

Snowling, S. and Hulme, C. (2003) *Dyslexia* 9(2): 1127–33.

Solity, J. (1996) Discrepancy definition of dyslexia: an assessment through teaching perspective, *Educational Psychology in Practice*, 12(3): 141–51.

Springer, S.P. and Deutsch, G. (1998) *Left Brain, Right Brain*. New York: W.H. Freeman.

Stahl, S.A. (2002) Different strokes for different folks?, in L. Abbeduto (ed.) *Taking Sides: Clashing on Controversial Issues in Educational Psychology* (pp. 98, 107). Guilford, CT: McGraw-Hill.

Stanovich, K.E., Siegel, L.S. and Gottardo, A. (1997) Subtypes of developmental dyslexia: differences in phonological and orthographic coding, in B.A. Blachman (ed.) *Foundations of Reading Acquisition and Dyslexia: Implications for Early Intervention*. Mahwah, NJ: Lawrence Erlbaum Associates, Inc.

Stanovich, K.E. and Stanovich, P.J. (1997) Further thoughts on aptitude/achievement discrepancy, *Educational Psychology in Practice*, 13(1): 3–8.

Stein, J. and Walsh, V. (1997) To see but not to read: the magnocellular theory of dyslexia, *Trends in Neuroscience*, 2: 147–52.

Tallal, P., Miller, S L., Jenkins, W.M. and Merzenich, M.M. (1997) The role of processing in temporal language-based disorders: research and clinical implications, in B.A. Blachman (ed.) *Foundations of Reading Acquisition and Dyslexia: Implications for Early Intervention*. Mahwah, NJ: Lawrence Erlbaum Associates, Inc.

Topping, K. (2001) *Thinking, Reading, Writing: A Practical Guide to Paired Learning with Peers, Parents, and Volunteers*. New York and London: Continuum International.

Turner, M. (2008) *Dyslexia Portfolio*. Swindon: GL Assessment.

Turner, M. and Smith, P. (2006) *Dyslexia Screener*. Windsor: NFER.

Warnock Report (1978) London: HMSO.

Watts–Vernon Reading Tests (1947) Slough: National Foundation for Educational Research.

Wechsler, D. (2003) *Wechsler Intelligence Scale for Children*, 4th edn. London: Harcourt.

West, T.G. (1997) *In the Mind's Eye: Visual Thinkers, Gifted People with Dyslexia and Other Learning Difficulties*. New York: Prometheus Books.

Wilkins, A. (1995) *Visual Stress*. Oxford: Oxford Publications.

Wilkinson, G.S. (1994) *Wide Range Achievement Tests*. Washington and Delaware: Wide Range Incorporated.

Wing, L. (1996) *The Autistic Spectrum: A Guide for Parents and Professionals*. London: Constable.

Wing, L. (2001) *The Autistic Spectrum*. London: Ulysses Press.

Zatz, S. and Chassin, L. (1985) Cognitions of test-anxious children under naturalistic test-taking conditions, *Journal of Consulting and Clinical Psychology*, 53(3): 393–401.

Index